THE GUIDE TO

MAINE

GOLF COURSES

By Park M. Morrison

Down East Books
Camden, Maine

Copyright © 2000 by Park Morrison
ISBN 0-89272-494-3
Book design by Michael Schroeder
Printed and bound by Versa Press, Inc.; East Preoria, Illinois

5 4 3 2 1

Down East Books
P.O. Box 679
Camden, ME 04843

BOOK ORDERS: 1-800-685-7962

LIBRARY OF CONGRESS CATALOGING-IN-PUBLICATION DATA

Morrison, Park M. (Park McLeod). 1955-
    The guide to Maine golf courses / by Park M. Morrison.
       p. cm.
    ISBN 0-89272-494-3 (trade paper)
    1. Golf courses—Maine—Directories. 2. Golf Courses—Maine—
    Guidebooks. I. Title.
    GV982.M2M67 2000
    796.352'06'8741—dc21
                                                            99-087083

For Missy, Storrey, and Sarah—
the best gallery a golfer ever had.

And for my father, Victor—
the best golf partner a son ever had.

ACKNOWLEDGMENTS

One of the reasons I took on this project was because the prospect of playing every golf course in the state of Maine in the name of "editorial research" was just too good to pass up. But Maine is a big state and there are a lot of golf courses. While I did get to play a majority of the layouts included here, I had to pass on more than a few. For that reason I relied on golf cart tours and interviews with club owners, superintendents, local pros and members to help with course descriptions. The list of people who assisted through their courtesy on site and those who helped over the phone is far too long to print here. But to all of them I am forever grateful.

Thanks also to folks at the Maine State Golf Association, especially Nancy DeFrancesco and Romeo Laberge, who are themselves walking and talking Maine golf guides; the Maine Golf Course Superintendents Association, who provided me my first foray into public speaking; and the researchers at the United States Golf Association who helped clarify, among other things, that it is indeed "green fee" not "greens fee."

From the non-golf side my thanks go to the staff at Down East Books, in particular my editor Chris Cornell, as much for his faith and patience as his editorial guidance. And to Mike Schroeder at Write Angle Communications who is as adept at publication design as he is with a wedge from 100 yards.

Finally, I'd like to thank my family. Without their overwhelming support—not to mention all those golf balls for my birthday and Christmas—this project would not nearly have been as much fun.

Preface

A tolerable day, a tolerable green, a tolerable opponent,

supply, or ought to supply, all that any reasonably constituted

human being should require in the way of entertainment.

— A. J. Balfour, The Humours of Golf

When hearing I was writing a guide to Maine golf courses, friends and acquaintances often asked, "Which one is the best?" or "Which one is your favorite?" I responded quickly and truthfully, "There isn't one," and referred to a comment made by Jim Dodson in his book *Final Rounds.* He said, "In good company there is no such thing as a bad golf course." And I believe that. In fact, I'd go as far as to say that my favorite course is the last one I played. That's the attitude I take with golf and the one I've taken with this book.

In Maine there are a wide variety of golf courses—from hidden gems to renowned resort courses, from lush well-manicured layouts to rough hardscrabble tracks where the superintendent, club pro, and night waterman are all the same person. Sure, some courses are "better" than others. But golf is a great equalizer. You still need to knock a little white ball into a four-and-a-half-inch-diameter hole. That's roughly the way it started five-hundred-plus years ago and is how it continues today. Whether you're Tiger Woods or Annika Sorenstam or a weekend hacker, the rules are the same. And because of that, whether you're playing Sugarloaf/USA or Great Cove, you can still experience the same enjoyment, frustrations, and rewards.

In his autobiography, *A Golfer's Life,* Arnold Palmer says, "Every golf course is going to be great to somebody for some reason or another." And it could be any number of reasons.

I grew up in a small town in Connecticut. When I first started playing, there was one nine-hole course in town. Built in the 1920s and remodeled in the 1950s, it was typical of its vintage. Holes followed the lay of the land. Greens were small, and irrigation was limited to a lawn sprinkler and a hundred feet of garden hose. In summer I played there every day with my best friend. We always wore shorts and usually played barefoot (best for feeling out golf balls along the edge of ponds). It's where I took my first golf lessons, where I won the club's junior golf championship, and where I witnessed my best friend's first hole in one.

In 1968 a new Robert Trent Jones–designed eighteen-hole championship golf course opened in town. My father was one of the founders of the club, and I spent high school and college summers working on the greens crew. I won the club's junior championship its first year (against meager competition, I must confess). I liked the new course with its broad, lush fairways and comparatively huge greens. It was a good deal longer and much more challenging than the "other" course. I was fortunate enough to be able to play both on a regular basis.

My point is that today, more than thirty years later, when I go back home to visit my father, golf is always on the agenda. And since he is still a member of both clubs, we'll get in at least one round at each. But as much as I look forward to playing the course that my father put years of effort into creating, that was designed by one of the best golf-course architects of this century, and that's considered by many one of the best golf courses in the state, I'm still drawn to that little nine-hole track with its tiny greens and burned-out fairways and a lifetime of memories. Arnold Palmer was right. In my mind that's a great golf course.

Similar stories abound for every golf course in Maine—if not the country. Half a dozen eighteen-hole golf courses have been built in this state since 1995. All were certainly multimillion-dollar projects. But for every Belgrade Lakes, Dunegrass, or Point Sebago there's a Western View, Old Orchard Beach, or Naples. And while the former receive well-deserved accolades, the latter will most often get the nostalgia vote. Unlike its beginnings, golf is no longer a rich man's game. It is a game for the masses. Its popularity has grown tremendously, especially in the last decade. As golf has evolved in America, it has become a game of memories. And the golf course, while important to the play, is only one piece of the enjoyment puzzle.

Golf in Maine – A Brief History

THE GAME OF GOLF has been played in Maine nearly as long as it has been played in America. Not long after a group of men led by Robert Lockhart and John Reid teed off on a Yonkers, New York, cow pasture in 1888, summer rusticators—those pioneers of our modern-day leisure class—caught the golfing bug and established golfing grounds at their down east retreats. Locals were certainly involved, although it was those "from away" who had the resources and abundance of free time to organize formal clubs. Most were ostensibly established to meet the demands of this growing leisure class in its pursuit of "sports, amusements and social contacts." Well connected and enormously wealthy, club organizers could attract the most talented men in the fledgling business of golf-course design—such as H. C. Leeds, Willie Park Jr., and Donald Ross—to oversee construction of proper layouts.

From Kennebunkport to Portland to Poland Spring to Bar Harbor, courses were being built at such a regular clip that by the early part of the twentieth century there were no fewer than thirty golf courses in the state. Virtually all were private, nine-hole affairs built on abandoned farm fields or meadows amid the hills, rocks, and thick spruce forests that characterize the Maine

Tufts Archives/Given Memorial Library

As Maine's reputation as a summer destination grew, prominent golfers of the day—such as Walter Hagen, shown here at Kebo Valley in 1922—often played exhibitions or local tournaments.

landscape. Although some no longer exist—victims of world wars, the economy, or waning interest—many survive today, some little changed from their original routing but modernized to the extent that technology, agronomy, and budgets allow. (Most, too, have abandoned their private charters in favor of semiprivate status.)

In the hundred or so years since those first courses were built, there have been similar building binges in Maine. These surges can be easily linked to the popularity of particular golfers of the day: Bobby Jones in the 1920s, Arnold Palmer in the 1960s, and Tiger Woods in the 1990s. The result is a pleasantly eclectic collection of dozens of golf courses that touch on every aspect of the historical spectrum.

While the New England region itself lays claim to some of the oldest continually operated golf courses in the country, Maine is home to a few of the oldest in New England. Kebo Valley Club in Bar Harbor (recognized as the eighth oldest in the United States) was organized in 1888 and had an original six-hole layout in play by 1892. A full nine holes was opened by 1896. Across Frenchman Bay in Winter Harbor a wealthy Philadelphia contingent established a summer colony at Grindstone Neck and, in 1895, built a nine-hole course that, while subsequently reorganized and lengthened, still traverses the same ground the club's founders played on more than a hundred years ago.

During the same decade summer communities in Northeast Harbor (Northeast Harbor Golf Club, 1895), Castine (Castine Golf Club, 1897), Kennebunkport (Cape Arundel Golf Club, 1897), and Islesboro (Tarratine Golf Club, 1896) also established golf clubs that are still active today.

The golf course at Poland Spring, shown here circa 1915, is reputed to be the oldest resort course in the United States. During its heyday, the resort attracted vistors from around the world.

Aside from Kebo Valley, the best-known course to come out of the latter part of the nineteenth century was Poland Spring Country Club—reputed to be the first, and thereby the oldest, resort course in the United States. Built on the grounds of the three-hundred-room Poland Spring House, a turn-of-the-century spa noted for the medicinal effects of its nearby springwaters, the original course was laid out by one Arthur H. Fenn, who at the time (1896) was an accomplished golfer and course architect. While the Poland Spring House attracted its share of the rich and famous from around the world, Poland Spring's golf course entertained its share of renowned golfers, including Harry Vardon and a young Bobby Jones. With Maine's growing reputation as a summer destination, other prominent golfers of the time, such as Walter Hagen and Gene Sarazen, often played exhibitions or local tournaments.

Arthur Fenn was one of many prominent architects (Willie Park Jr. and Walter Travis were others) affiliated with early Maine golf. Certainly the best known was Donald Ross, who designed more than five hundred courses in his career, including the famed No. 2 course at Pinehurst, North Carolina, and Oak Hill in New York.

Ross had a hand in designing or remodeling no fewer than ten courses in Maine. Some of his best efforts—Augusta Country Club and Portland Country Club—remain private, but you'll get a good taste of the Ross style at Biddeford-Saco, Cape Neddick, Lake Kezar, Lucerne-in-Maine, Northeast Harbor, Penobscot Valley, or Poland Spring (where in 1913 he remodeled and added to Arthur Fenn's design). Some of these tracks have been altered over the years, but Ross's influence is very much in evidence.

Other architects who have had a significant impact on the Maine golf landscape include the teams of Wayne Stiles and John Van Kleek, Eugene and Phil Wogan, and most recently Geoffrey Cornish and Brian Silva. During the 1990s, other notables such as Robert Trent Jones Jr. (Sugarloaf/USA) and Dan Maples (Dunegrass) added their creativity to the mix. Ogunquit-based designer William Bradley Booth (The Ledges, The Meadows, Spring Meadows) is one of a new generation of architects who have started to make their marks as we enter a new century.

THROUGH THE 1920s golf-course design and construction in Maine were primarily limited to "rich people from away." The subsequent depression and world war put a virtual halt to new projects. It wasn't until the 1960s, when television made Arnold Palmer a national hero, that Maine's second building boom hit high gear. During that decade thirty new courses were opened. Interestingly, however, most weren't built by wealthy out-of-state developers: The majority were local enterprises, and many were started by people who had no previous experience with golf at all.

Typical of this era of construction is the story of Natanis Golf Club in Vassalboro. In the early 1960s Paul Browne decided to cut back his dairy farm business, converting existing farmland into a golf course. His knowledge of golf-course design was scant, but he figured he knew how to grow grass and had enough Maine-bred determination that failure was not an option.

With help and advice from local golf pros, Natanis's first nine holes opened in 1965. The first greens were built in the shape of Maine counties. Today, thirty-five years later, that original nine has grown to twenty-seven, with nine more (designed by Dan Maples, based in Pinehurst, North Carolina) scheduled to open in 2000. At thirty-six holes, it will be the largest golf facility north of Boston. In 1996 *Golf Digest* ranked Natanis as one of the top five hundred public courses in the country. More than fifty thousand rounds were played there in 1998. But more impressive than just numbers and five-star ratings is the fact that the golf course is still owned and operated by the Browne family.

Stories like the Brownes' are not rare in Maine. From Va Jo Wa in Island Falls to Palmyra to Rivermeadow in Westbrook, family-owned and -operated golf courses dot the landscape. They succeed because of their owners' love for the game and commitment to providing the best golf experience possible. Although hard work is a major factor, a certain amount of credit for their success should go to the Maine State Golf Association (MSGA), the Maine Golf Course Superintendents Association (MGCSA), and the Maine Chapter of the New England PGA. All three groups are affiliated with national organizations and provide technical and management advice for golf-course owners.

THE MOST RECENT BUILDING BOOM has taken Maine golf to another level. Interestingly, most courses are still being built by locals, although their price tags have gone up significantly. With golf's popularity—and stricter environmental rules—multimillion-dollar projects are the norm. The trend now is toward larger and potentially more profitable eighteen-hole layouts. Not only is the quantity increasing, but the quality of golf courses in Maine is on the rise, too. New courses are raising the bar, and established nine-hole layouts are keeping pace. Several course expansions opened for play in 1999, and more are slated to be completed by 2000.

The results of this recent surge have put Maine on the golfing destination map. Sugarloaf/USA and Sable Oaks debuted in the early 1990s; Point Sebago, Dunegrass, Belgrade Lakes, and The Ledges have since joined them as Maine's premier golf venues. Add to these the early standard-bearers—Bethel Inn, Samoset Resort, and Kebo Valley Club—and you have as fine a collection of golf courses as exists anywhere in the Northeast, if not the country.

And that's just for starters. There are more than 120 golf courses in the state of Maine. Each has its own personality and charm. From small seaside tracks to majestic mountaintop layouts, it is an impressive cast of characters. But the list doesn't stop here. As this guide is being written, at least two new eighteen-hole golf courses are under construction (the Links at Outlook, Spring Meadows), a few more are in the permitting stage, and an untold number have yet to be announced. Interestingly, golf in Maine ends this century as it began, at the forefront of the latest golf boom.

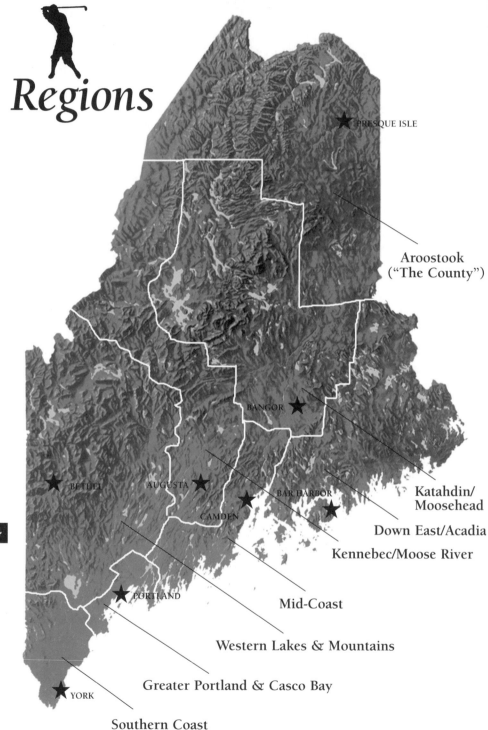

Regions

PRESQUE ISLE

Aroostook
("The County")

BANGOR

BETHEL

AUGUSTA

BAR HARBOR

CAMDEN

Katahdin/
Moosehead

Down East/Acadia

Kennebec/Moose River

PORTLAND

Mid-Coast

Western Lakes & Mountains

Greater Portland & Casco Bay

YORK

Southern Coast

To help you in planning your golfing activity in Maine, I have broken the state into geographical regions—the same used by the Maine Office of Tourism. These are delineated both in the large map on the facing page and in the smaller, individual maps accompanying the description of each region, below.

SOUTHERN COAST

The gateway to Maine, the state's Southern Coast stretches from the Piscataqua River and Kittery to Old Orchard Beach, then west to the New Hampshire border. History abounds in this area, which was first settled in 1636, not long after the Pilgrims established their colony at Plymouth, Massachusetts. Noted mostly for its large sandy beaches (Old Orchard Beach is seven miles long), this region's inland villages boast quintessential New England charm. Its proximity to Boston and points south has made the Southern Coast a popular destination for out-of-state visitors. Golfers have been the beneficiaries: Two new championship eighteen-hole layouts opened in 1999, and another is scheduled to open in 2000.

BIDDEFORD-SACO GOLF CLUB	*Saco*
CAPE ARUNDEL GOLF CLUB	*Kennebunkport*
CAPE NEDDICK COUNTRY CLUB	*Cape Neddick*
DUNEGRASS GOLF CLUB	*Old Orchard Beach*
DUTCH ELM GOLF CLUB	*Arundel*
GOLF AT PROVINCE LAKE	*Parsonfield*
HIGHLAND LINKS GOLF CLUB	*York*
THE LEDGES GOLF CLUB	*York*
THE LINKS AT OUTLOOK	*Berwick*
OLD ORCHARD BEACH COUNTRY CLUB	*Old Orchard Beach*
PINE HOLLOW LITTLE PAR 3	*Sanford*
SALMON FALLS COUNTRY CLUB	*Hollis*
SANFORD COUNTRY CLUB	*Sanford*
WEBHANNET GOLF CLUB	*Kennebunk Beach*
WEST NEWFIELD GOLF COURSE	*West Newfield*

GREATER PORTLAND AREA

Not only Maine's largest city, Portland is also the state's cultural hub. Downtown's Old Port section is a picturesque collection of nineteenth-century brick buildings that today house small shops, art galleries, and restaurants. Museums and historical sites are scattered throughout the metropolitan area. One of the country's oldest lighthouses, Portland Head Light (built in 1791) stands sentinel at the entrance to its busy harbor. Casco Bay and its islands are accessible by regular ferry service from the Portland waterfront. Encompassing an area south to Scarborough, north to Freeport, and west to Gorham, Greater Portland has the highest concentration of golf courses in Maine. Though located in Maine's busiest city, their tranquil beauty often belies their setting.

FREEPORT COUNTRY CLUB	*Freeport*
GORHAM COUNTRY CLUB	*Gorham*
NONESUCH RIVER GOLF CLUB	*Scarborough*
PLEASANT HILL GOLF CLUB	*Scarborough*
RIVERMEADOW GOLF CLUB	*Westbrook*
RIVERSIDE MUNICIPAL GOLF COURSE	*Portland*
SABLE OAKS GOLF CLUB	*South Portland*
SOUTH PORTLAND MUNICIPAL GOLF COURSE	*South Portland*
SPRING MEADOWS GOLF & COUNTRY CLUB	*Gray*
TWIN FALLS GOLF CLUB	*Westbrook*
VAL HALLA GOLF CLUB	*Cumberland*
WESTERLY WINDS GOLF COURSE	*Westbrook*
WILLOWDALE GOLF CLUB	*Scarborough*

WESTERN LAKES AND MOUNTAINS

The region known as the Western Lakes and Mountains covers an area from Sebago Lake (Maine's second largest and most popular) north through the foothills of the White Mountains. Dominated by rolling farm fields, dense hardwood forests, and pristine lakes, western Maine is more rustic than—but every bit as alluring as—its coastal counterparts. The dramatic terrain serves as a backdrop to some of the most spectacular golf courses in the state. Carved through thick woodlands, these tracks offer great variety in appealing North Woods fashion.

ALLEN MOUNTAIN GOLF COURSE	*Denmark*
APPLE VALLEY GOLF CLUB	*Lewiston*
BETHEL INN & COUNTRY CLUB	*Bethel*
BRIDGTON HIGHLANDS COUNTRY CLUB	*Bridgton*
FAIRLAWN GOLF & COUNTRY CLUB	*Poland*
FRYE ISLAND GOLF COURSE	*Frye Island*
LAKE KEZAR COUNTRY CLUB	*Lovell*
MAPLE LANE INN & GOLF CLUB	*Livermore Falls*
MINGO SPRINGS GOLF COURSE	*Rangeley*
NAPLES GOLF CLUB	*Naples*
NORWAY COUNTRY CLUB	*Norway*
OAKDALE GOLF CLUB	*Mexico*

MID-COAST REGION

Stretching from Brunswick to Searsport, the Mid-Coast Region is best known for its maritime past. The shipbuilding towns of Bath, Camden, and Searsport have turned out everything from *America*'s Cup racers, to four-, five-, and six-masted schooners to modern-day battleships. Today the area's maritime heritage is continued through a vibrant windjammer fleet that explores the myriad islands of Penobscot Bay. The rocky coastline here is dotted with bustling resort towns and small fishing villages, providing idyllic backdrops to some of the state's premier golf venues.

BATH COUNTRY CLUB	*Bath*
BOOTHBAY COUNTRY CLUB	*Boothbay*
BRUNSWICK GOLF CLUB	*Brunswick*
COUNTRY VIEW GOLF CLUB	*Brooks*
GOOSE RIVER GOLF CLUB	*Rockport*
MERE CREEK GOLF COURSE	*Brunswick*
NORTH HAVEN GOLF CLUB	*North Haven*
NORTHPORT GOLF CLUB	*Northport*
ROCKLAND GOLF CLUB	*Rockland*
SAMOSET RESORT GOLF CLUB	*Rockport*
SEARSPORT PINES GOLF COURSE	*Searsport*
SHORE ACRES GOLF CLUB	*Sebasco Estates*
STREAMSIDE GOLF COURSE	*Winterport*
WAWENOCK COUNTRY CLUB	*Walpole*

ACADIA/DOWN EAST

Mt. Desert Island has been Maine's most popular destination for both in- and out-of-state visitors since the turn of the century. Today Acadia National Park and the town of Bar Harbor are its biggest draws. Hiking, canoeing, whale-watching, and shopping are just a few of the area's many attractions. Golf has long been a popular activity here, and as a result the area is home to some of the oldest and most picturesque courses in the state.

BAR HARBOR GOLF CLUB	*Trenton*
BLINK BONNIE GOLF CLUB	*Sorrento*
BUCKSPORT GOLF COURSE	*Bucksport*
CASTINE GOLF CLUB	*Castine*
CAUSEWAY GOLF CLUB	*Southwest Harbor*
GREAT COVE GOLF CLUB	*Roque Bluffs*
GRINDSTONE NECK GOLF COURSE	*Winter Harbor*
ISLAND COUNTRY CLUB	*Sunset*
KEBO VALLEY CLUB	*Bar Harbor*
LUCERNE-IN-MAINE GOLF COURSE	*Lucerne-in-Maine*
NORTHEAST HARBOR GOLF CLUB	*Northeast Harbor*
ST. CROIX COUNTRY CLUB	*Calais*
WHITE BIRCHES GOLF CLUB	*Ellsworth*

KATAHDIN/MOOSEHEAD REGION

Encompassing Maine's largest lake (Moosehead) and the state's highest mountain (Mt. Katahdin), this region is known for its majestic beauty. Bangor, northern Maine's largest city, is a center for the region's business and cultural activities. Timber and farming are the major industries; as a result the golf courses here, as in other portions of northern Maine, have a more laid-back ambiance.

BANGOR MUNICIPAL GOLF CLUB	*Bangor*
CARMEL VALLEY GOLF LINKS	*Carmel*
DEXTER MUNICIPAL GOLF CLUB	*Dexter*
FELT BROOK GOLF CENTER	*Holden*
FOXCROFT GOLF CLUB	*Dover-Foxcroft*
GREEN VALLEY GOLF CLUB	*Enfield*

HAMPDEN COUNTRY CLUB	*Hampden*
HERMON MEADOWS GOLF CLUB	*Hermon*
HIDDEN MEADOWS GOLF COURSE	*Old Town*
HILLCREST GOLF CLUB	*Millinocket*
JATO HIGHLANDS GOLF CLUB	*Lincoln*
KATAHDIN COUNTRY CLUB	*Milo*
KENDUSKEAG VALLEY GOLF COURSE	*Kenduskeag*
MT. KINEO GOLF COURSE	*Rockwood*
ORCHARD VIEW GOLF CLUB	*Newport*
PENOBSCOT VALLEY COUNTRY CLUB	*Orono*
PINE HILL GOLF CLUB	*Brewer*
PISCATAQUIS COUNTRY CLUB	*Guilford*
SQUAW MOUNTAIN VILLAGE GOLF COURSE	*Greenville Junction*
TODD VALLEY COUNTRY CLUB	*Charleston*
WHITETAIL GOLF COURSE	*Charleston*

KENNEBEC/MOOSE RIVER REGION

 This region includes Maine's capital, Augusta, and follows the Kennebec River through central Maine's lake district amid fertile farmland and rolling hills and mountains until it reaches the Canadian border near Jackman. Historically, the river has been a symbol of the economic vitality of the region. Whereas in the past it was used to ferry lumber to mills along its length, today it carries a different commodity—people—who flock in large numbers to enjoy white-water rafting adventures. Golf continues to be a popular activity in the area, as evidenced by recent construction.

BELGRADE LAKES GOLF COURSE	*Belgrade Lakes*
CAPITOL CITY GOLF COURSE	*Augusta*
CEDAR SPRINGS GOLF COURSE	*Albion*
COBBOSSEE COLONY GOLF COURSE	*Monmouth*
J. W. PARKS GOLF CLUB	*Pittsfield*
KENNEBEC HEIGHTS COUNTRY CLUB	*Farmingdale*
LAKEVIEW GOLF CLUB	*Burnham*
LAKEWOOD GOLF CLUB	*Madison*
LOONS COVE GOLF COURSE	*Skowhegan*
THE MEADOWS GOLF CLUB	*Litchfield*
MOOSE RIVER GOLF CLUB	*Jackman*
NATANIS GOLF CLUB	*Vassalboro*
PALMYRA GOLF COURSE	*Palmyra*
PINE RIDGE MUNICIPAL GOLF COURSE	*Waterville*

SPRINGBROOK GOLF CLUB	*Leeds*
WATERVILLE COUNTRY CLUB	*Waterville*
WESTERN VIEW GOLF CLUB	*Augusta*

AROOSTOOK

Maine's largest (sixty-five hundred square miles) and northern-most county, Aroostook is best known for its rich farmland. Potatoes have been the dominant crop, and not surprisingly, former potato fields lend themselves quite nicely to the broad, rolling fairways that typify the area's golf courses. Hills and woodlands provide beautiful backdrops to some of the state's least-crowded courses.

AROOSTOOK VALLEY COUNTRY CLUB	*Fort Fairfield*
BIRCH POINT GOLF CLUB	*St. David*
CARIBOU COUNTRY CLUB	*Caribou*
FORT KENT GOLF CLUB	*Fort Kent*
HOULTON COMMUNITY GOLF COURSE	*Houlton*
LIMESTONE COUNTRY CLUB	*Limestone*
MARS HILL COUNTRY CLUB	*Mars Hill*
PORTAGE HILLS COUNTRY CLUB	*Portage*
PRESQUE ISLE COUNTRY CLUB	*Presque Isle*
VA JO WA GOLF COURSE	*Island Falls*

Using This Guide

The purpose of this book is not to rank Maine's golf courses but rather to give you enough information to assess the kind of experience you might have at each one. It is not for me to say what course is better than another; too many subjective factors come into play. I try to stay out of the rating game. I'll leave that up to the editors at *Golf* and *Golf Digest*.

With that in mind, I've compiled here what I believe is a comprehensive inventory of golf in Maine. Starting on page 23, the courses are listed alphabetically throughout the guide. The information provided is as up to date as possible given book-publishing lead time. Using the guide should be fairly straight-forward, but let me clarify some of the terms used in each description:

REGION: One of the geographical areas described on pages 15 through 20.

MAP: Relates to the corresponding map in DeLorme's *Maine Atlas & Gazetteer* [telephone 800-452-5931], an excellent resource when traveling the state by car.

ESTABLISHED: The year the club was established. In many cases, the golf course itself opened for play later.

NUMBER OF HOLES: At present Maine has more nine-hole layouts than eighteen-hole courses. That's changing as more existing courses expand. If an expansion is in the works, it is noted here.

COURSE LENGTH/PAR: Most eighteen-hole golf courses have three sets of tees, but a few have more, and some nine-hole courses have fewer. For consistency, I've chosen to list the Back, the championship tees or "tips"; Middle, the regular men's tees; and Front, the regular ladies' tees. Where only two sets of tees exist—men's and ladies'—I've simply called them Back and Front. The yardage and par listed represent the total for eighteen holes.

COURSE RATING/SLOPE: Through its state chapters, the United States Golf Association (USGA) establishes course and slope ratings for golf courses. As defined in the USGA's Handicap System Manual, **COURSE RATING** "indicates the evaluation of the playing difficulty of a course for scratch golfers under normal course and weather conditions. It is expressed as strokes taken to one decimal place, and is based on yardage and other obstacles to the extent that they affect the scoring ability of a scratch golfer."

The **SLOPE RATING** "indicates the measurement of the relative difficulty of a course for players who are not scratch golfers compared to the Course Rating (i.e. compared to the difficulty of the course for scratch golfers). The lowest possible slope rating is 55, and the highest is 155. A golf course of standard playing difficulty has a USGA Slope Rating of 113."

Developed as a handicapping tool, slope also helps golfers determine the relative difficulty of a course. For example, Wawenock Country Club in Walpole plays to a par 70 and has a course rating of 69.0. The same is true of Kebo Valley Club in Bar Harbor. However, Kebo's slope rating is 130, as compared to Wawenock's 120. Though you wouldn't be able to tell from the course ratings, due to its higher slope rating Kebo is likely to play a little tougher for the "non-scratch" golfer than Wawenock.

Head Professional: This indicates a PGA-certified professional is on staff.

Course Architect: The designer(s) of record. Where known, I've added designations O9, A9, and R—meaning "original nine," "added nine," and "remodeled," respectively.

Golf Facilities: The choices are full pro shop, driving range, practice green, practice bunker, club rental, club repair, club storage, cart rental, pull-cart rental, instruction, golf school, locker room, showers, restaurant, snack bar, caddies, lounge, and accommodations.

Tee Times: If you know where and when you want to play, it's best to call ahead during the peak season, regardless of whether tee times are required.

How Long in Advance: How many days in advance tee-time reservations will be accepted. Included only if tee times are necessary or recommended.

Ranger: Most course staffs include someone who monitors the speed of play. A "yes" here means that this position is staffed full time in season.

Tee-Off Interval Time: Typically eight minutes, but a few courses spread this out depending on weather and the season. Included only if tee times are necessary or recommended.

Time to Play 18 Holes: This is an average time as supplied by the club.

Earliest Tee-Off: For nonmembers, this is generally when the pro shop opens.

Green Fees: Obviously, prices change. For this reason I've grouped green fees into ranges:

> **$** = less than $20
> **$$** = $20–29
> **$$$** = $30–39
> **$$$$** = $40 and above

Note: Prices listed are eighteen-hole, in-season fees. Many courses offer weekly specials and late-afternoon discounts. Fees are lower during off-season months.

Payment: Are credit cards accepted? If so, which ones?

Season: Maine golfers are an enthusiastic bunch. In most cases, courses open up as soon after snowmelt as possible. Most accept players through October, and a few stay open till the first snow.

Local Chamber of Commerce: Need a place to stay? A restaurant suggestion? Here's the place to start.

Local Attractions: Points of interest to visiting golfers and their families.

Directions: Travel information assumes you are coming into Maine from the south.

Course Description: A general overview of the course layout with the emphasis on its more interesting holes. Course history and anecdotes are included as available.

Courses Nearby: A list of courses that are within a reasonable drive of the links being described. Obviously, in the more rural parts of the state a "reasonable drive" might be a little longer than one in more populated areas.

Courses

ALLEN MOUNTAIN GOLF COURSE

BUSH ROW ROAD
DENMARK
207-452-2282
E-MAIL: allenmt@pivot.net
REGION: Western Lakes and Mountains
MAP: 4
ESTABLISHED: 1995
NUMBER OF HOLES: 9
COURSE LENGTH/PAR: Back: 5,061/70   **Front:** 4,472/70
COURSE RATING/SLOPE: Back: 65.7/114 **Front:** 66.7/114
HEAD PROFESSIONAL: No
COURSE ARCHITECT: Peter Chase
GOLF FACILITIES: Club rental, cart rental, pull-cart rental, snack bar
TEE TIMES: Not necessary
RANGER: No
TIME TO PLAY 18 HOLES: 4 hours, 30 minutes
EARLIEST TEE-OFF: 7 a.m.
GREEN FEES: Weekends (18): $ Weekdays (18): $
PAYMENT: Cash only
SEASON: May 15 through October 15
LOCAL CHAMBER OF COMMERCE: Bridgton-Lakes Region, 207-647-3472
LOCAL ATTRACTIONS: Nearby lakes for swimming, fishing, and boating
DIRECTIONS: Take Route 117 to Denmark Village, then drive 2½ miles south to the end of Bush Row Road.
COURSE DESCRIPTION: Referred to as "a miniature Sugarloaf" for its spectacular views and severe elevation changes, Allen Mountain was designed and built in 1995 by Peter Chase and family. Cut through thick woods, the course is charac-

terized by narrow fairways that put a premium on shot placement. It can play tougher than its 114 slope rating because of elevation changes—from a low of 850 feet above sea level to 1,150 feet. The course winds its way up the mountain to the signature fifth hole, a 168-yard par-3, noted as much for the view from the tee as for the finesse required to drop your tee shot on the small green.

COURSES NEARBY: Bridgton Highlands, Naples

APPLE VALLEY GOLF CLUB
316 PINEWOODS ROAD
LEWISTON
207-784-9773
REGION: Western Lakes and Mountains
MAP: 11
ESTABLISHED: 1963
NUMBER OF HOLES: 9
COURSE LENGTH/PAR: Back: 5,035/70   **Front:** 4,703/72
COURSE RATING/SLOPE: Back: 63.7/111 **Front:** 66.8/109
HEAD PROFESSIONAL: Yes
COURSE ARCHITECT: NA
GOLF FACILITIES: Pro shop, practice green, club rental, club repair, cart rental, pull-cart rental, snack bar, lounge
TEE TIMES: Not necessary
RANGER: Yes
TIME TO PLAY 18 HOLES: 4 hours
EARLIEST TEE-OFF: 7 a.m.
GREEN FEES: Weekend (18): $ **Weekday (18): $**
PAYMENT: Cash only
SEASON: April 15 through November 15
LOCAL CHAMBER OF COMMERCE: Androscoggin County, 207-783-2249
LOCAL ATTRACTIONS: Bates College, Range Ponds State Park (Poland Spring), Shaker Museum (New Gloucester)
DIRECTIONS: Take Exit 13 off the Maine Turnpike (I-495). Follow Route 196 East toward
Lisbon. In about 3/4 mile you'll see Pinewood Road on your right. Follow signs to the course.
COURSE DESCRIPTION: Located just east of Lewiston, this is a fairly flat, open track and therefore easy to walk. Built in the 1960s, its current owners have over the past 15 years done major renovations, including several new tees, bunkers, and drainage work that have improved play and added to the course's challenge. Four ponds come into play on seven holes, so there is ample opportunity to get wet. Two great par-3s highlight this layout. The 147-yard third plays over water to an hourglass-shaped green with a bunker in front and a severe slope to the left.

The green on the short 108-yard fifth sits on a knoll with a bunker right and a pot bunker left. The course is complemented by the clubhouse—a 200-year-old post-and-beam farmhouse. The former carriage house has been converted into a lounge that seats 40 to 50 people.

COURSES NEARBY: The Meadows, Poland Spring, Prospect Hill, Springbrook, Turner Highlands

AROOSTOOK VALLEY COUNTRY CLUB

RUSSELL ROAD
FORT FAIRFIELD
207-476-8083
WEB: www.intellis.net/avcc
REGION: Aroostook
MAP: 65
ESTABLISHED: 1927
NUMBER OF HOLES: 18
COURSE LENGTH/PAR: Back: 6,304/72 **Middle:** 5,977/72 **Front:** 5,393/72
COURSE RATING/SLOPE: Back: 69.9/117 **Middle:** 68.4/113 **Front:** 70.0/119
HEAD PROFESSIONAL: Yes
COURSE ARCHITECT: Howard Watson
GOLF FACILITIES: Full pro shop, driving range, practice green, practice bunker, club rental, club repair, club storage, cart rental, pull-cart rental, instruction, locker room, showers, restaurant, snack bar, lounge
TEE TIMES: Recommended
HOW LONG IN ADVANCE: 3 days
RANGER: Yes
TEE-OFF INTERVAL TIME: 8 minutes
TIME TO PLAY 18 HOLES: 4 hours
EARLIEST TEE-OFF: 6 a.m.
GREEN FEES: Weekend (18): $$ **Weekday (18):** $$
PAYMENT: MasterCard, Visa
SEASON: April through September
LOCAL CHAMBER OF COMMERCE: Fort Fairfield, 207-472-3802
LOCAL ATTRACTIONS: Fort Fairfield block house, annual potato festivals
COURSE DESCRIPTION: Ironically, the best known of all Aroostook County area golf courses isn't even in the United States, let alone The County. Built in 1927 during Prohibition, club founders (both Americans and Canadians) skirted the issue by establishing the Aroostook Valley Country Club with a clubhouse and golf course on the Canadian side and a parking lot on the American side. Expanded to 18 holes in 1958, the course still maintains its international flavor. A hooked tee shot on number one will be not only out of bounds but also out of the country. Broad, rolling fairways lined with towering spruce and pine trees

frame well-contoured greens. Bunkers are plentiful. In most cases holes are straightforward but can be deceiving. The 510-yard par-5 fourteenth is a downhill dogleg left. A pond stretches immediately in front of the green, and if you leave your approach short, the slope to the elevated putting surface can be treacherous. Completing a great one-two punch is the 156-yard par-3 fifteenth: a large green surrounded by trees, guarded by bunkers and water. It's easy to see why the members have dubbed it Devil's Hole. A pro shop now exists on the U.S. side, and the parking lot has been divided between countries.

COURSES NEARBY: Caribou, Limestone, Mars Hill, Presque Isle

BANGOR MUNICIPAL GOLF CLUB
278 WEBSTER AVENUE
BANGOR
207-941-0232
REGION: Katahdin/Moosehead Region
MAP: 23
ESTABLISHED: 1964
NUMBER OF HOLES: 27
COURSE LENGTH/PAR: Back: 6,345/71   **Front:** 5,173/71
COURSE RATING/SLOPE: Back: 69.2/115 **Front:** 69.1/111
HEAD PROFESSIONAL: Yes
COURSE ARCHITECT: Geoffrey Cornish
GOLF FACILITIES: Full pro shop, driving range, practice green, club rental, club repair, cart rental, pull-cart rental, instruction, restaurant/snack bar, lounge
TEE TIMES: Not necessary
RANGER: Yes
TIME TO PLAY 18 HOLES: 4 hours
EARLIEST TEE-OFF: 7 a.m.
GREEN FEES: Weekend (18): $$ **Weekday (18):** $$
PAYMENT: MasterCard, Visa
SEASON: Mid-April through mid-November
LOCAL CHAMBER OF COMMERCE: Bangor Region, 207-947-0307
LOCAL ATTRACTIONS: Bangor Mall, Paul Bunyan Park, Stephen King home, Penobscot River cruises, University of Maine (Orono)
DIRECTIONS: Take Exit 46 off I-95. Turn right onto Norway Road, then right again onto Webster Street. Right on Webster. The course is on your left.
COURSE DESCRIPTION: A well-maintained course that's regarded as one of the best municipal facilities in the state. It's the only course in Maine to have held a USGA-sponsored event—the 1978 Public Links Championship. It is the site of the annual Bangor Open, and it most recently hosted the 1998 Maine Open. Large tees and greens—some of the largest in the state—and broad, rolling fairways make for some interesting challenges as well as accommodating a lot of play. The original 18, designed by Geoffrey Cornish in 1964, is an open layout with

mounds and bunkers guarding the greens. A new nine, designed by Cornish and partner Brian Silva, was opened in 1988. It is far tighter, with more extensive mounds and bunkers. Full irrigation was recently installed. It's a good layout for all handicap levels.

COURSES NEARBY: Carmel Valley, Felt Brook, Hampden, Hermon Meadows, Hidden Meadows, Kenduskeag, Lucerne-in-Maine, Penobscot Valley, Pine Hill

BAR HARBOR GOLF CLUB
ROUTES 3 AND 204
TRENTON
207-667-7505
REGION: Acadia/Down East
MAP: 16
ESTABLISHED: 1965
NUMBER OF HOLES: 18
COURSE LENGTH/PAR: Back: 6,680/71   **Middle:** 6,450/71   **Front:** 5,542/73
COURSE RATING/SLOPE: Back: 71.1/NA   **Middle:** 70.2/122   **Front:** 70.4/119
HEAD PROFESSIONAL: Yes
COURSE ARCHITECT: Philip Wogan
GOLF FACILITIES: Full pro shop, driving range, practice green, club rental, club repair, club storage, cart rental, pull-cart rental, instruction, restaurant, lounge
TEE TIMES: Not necessary
RANGER: Yes
TEE-OFF INTERVAL TIME: 8 minutes
TIME TO PLAY 18 HOLES: 4 hours, 30 minutes
EARLIEST TEE-OFF: 7 a.m.
GREEN FEES: Weekend (18): $$$ **Weekday (18): $$$**
PAYMENT: MasterCard, Visa
SEASON: Mid-April through October
LOCAL CHAMBER OF COMMERCE: Trenton, 207-288-3674
LOCAL ATTRACTIONS: Acadia National Park, Bar Harbor, whale-watching tours, boat excursions, wildlife
DIRECTIONS: From Ellsworth take Route 3 toward Mount Desert Island (Bar Harbor). After about 4 miles turn left onto Route 204. The club is on your right.
COURSE DESCRIPTION: Just 4 miles from Mount Desert Island, this low-lying links-style course offers great views of Acadia National Park's mountains. The layout is wide open, but fairway bunkers and rough narrow most landing areas. Similarly greens are well protected and water comes into play on a few holes. The Jordan River provides a pretty backdrop to the 388-yard par-4 second. A dogleg right, the hole plays downhill to a well-contoured green protected by a bunker to the right and a small gully left. From the tee at the 155-yard eleventh, the green appears to back right up to the river, but there's actually about 10 to 15 yards of

rough before you have to worry about water. The layout's rolling terrain and broad gullies will sometimes leave you with a downhill lie for an uphill approach to the green. Such is the case at the 405-yard sixteenth, the number one handicap hole, as well as the long par-5s at thirteen and eighteen (589 and 544 yards, respectively). Close to the ocean, there is generally a stiff sea breeze to contend with as well.

Courses Nearby: Causeway, Grindstone Neck, Kebo Valley, Northeast Harbor, White Birches

Bath Country Club

Whiskeag Road

Bath

207-442-8411

Web: www.bathcountryclub.com

Region: Mid-Coast Region

Map: 6

Established: 1932

Number of Holes: 18

Course Length/Par: Back: 6,216/70 **Middle:** 5,751/70 **Front:** 4,708/70

Course Rating/Slope: Back: 70.2/128 **Middle:** 67.8/123 **Front:** 67.0/115

Head Professional: Yes

Course Architect: Stiles & Van Kleek (O9), Cornish & Silva (A9)

Golf Facilities: Full pro shop, practice green, practice bunker, club rental, club repair, club storage, cart rental, pull-cart rental, instruction, locker room, restaurant, snack bar, lounge

Tee Times: Necessary

How Long in Advance: 7 days

Ranger: Yes

Tee-Off Interval Time: 8 minutes

Time to Play 18 Holes: 4 hours

Earliest Tee-Off: 7 a.m.

Green Fees: Weekend (18): $$ **Weekday (18):** $$

Payment: MasterCard, Visa, American Express

Season: April through October

Local Chamber of Commerce: Bath-Brunswick Region, 207-725-8797

Local Attractions: Maine Maritime Museum, Popham Beach State Park, Reid State Park, Bath Iron Works

Directions: From Route 1 take New Meadows Road—West Bath Exit. Turn right onto New Meadows and drive 1 mile to a stop sign (the road name changes to Ridge Road). Follow for another mile. Take a right onto Whiskeag. The club is on your left.

Course Description: The city of Bath is home to Bath Iron Works, which has built everything from *America*'s Cup racers to Aegis destroyers. Maine's maritime history is on display at the nearby Maine Maritime Museum. Designed by Stiles & Van Kleek (1932), the original nine holes at Bath were remodeled and a second nine added by Cornish & Silva in 1994. The result is a successful blend of old and new. The newer back side is tighter and hillier, with holes eleven through fifteen presenting the the most interesting challenge. Although short, they can prove the most difficult on the course. All but the par-3 thirteenth require a drive to carry a marsh that meanders through the property. On the 326-yard par-4 eleventh you need to not only clear the wetlands but land your tee shot beyond a 15-foot rock ledge that rises straight up from the fairway. Large, rolling greens add to the test. The clubhouse has been recently renovated and is a comfortable place to relax following a round.

COURSES NEARBY: Brunswick, Bath, Mere Creek, Shore Acres, Wawenock

BELGRADE LAKES GOLF COURSE

WEST ROAD
BELGRADE LAKES
207-495-4653
WEB: www.belgradelakesgolf.com
REGION: Kennebec/Moose River Region
MAP: 12
ESTABLISHED: 1998
NUMBER OF HOLES: 18
COURSE LENGTH/PAR: Back: 6,653/71   **Middle:** 6,138/71   **Front:** 4,881/71
COURSE RATING/SLOPE: Back: 71.6/142   **Middle:** 68.4/133   **Front:** 64.1/126
HEAD PROFESSIONAL: No
COURSE ARCHITECT: Clive Clark
GOLF FACILITIES: Full pro shop, practice green, club rental, pull-cart rental, snack bar, caddies
TEE TIMES: Necessary
RANGER: Yes
TEE-OFF INTERVAL TIME: 12 and 15 minutes
TIME TO PLAY 18 HOLES: 4 hours, 15 minutes
EARLIEST TEE-OFF: 7 a.m.
GREEN FEES: Weekend (18): $$$$ Weekday (18): $$$$
PAYMENT: MasterCard, Visa, American Express
SEASON: Mid-April through October
LOCAL CHAMBER OF COMMERCE: Mid-Maine, 207-873-3315 or 3316
LOCAL ATTRACTIONS: Belgrade Lakes region, hiking, camping
DIRECTIONS: Take Exit 31 off I-95. Follow Route 27 North about 12 miles to Belgrade Lakes. Turn left onto West Road (The Sunset Grill is on the corner). The golf course is 1/8 mile on your left.

COURSE DESCRIPTION: Designed by well-known British architect Clive Clark (his first course in the United States), Belgrade Lakes, whose full 18 opened in 1999, was recently named the 5th Best New Upscale Public Golf Course by *Golf Digest*. If you can get past the panoramic mountaintop view of nearby Great and Long Ponds, you arrive on the first tee for a treat suitable for golfers of all levels. Interestingly, only two holes—the first and tenth—present any significant elevation change on this hillside course. The rest subtly traverse the hilly terrain, making it walkable—albeit an active caddie program helps make that choice easier. The third hole, a 406-yard par-5 (469 yards from the tips), is a slight dogleg left that has large boulders (moved here during the clearing process) lining the entire right side of the fairway and water stretching up around the green to the left. The only consolation for an errant fade on this hole is that your ball is just as likely to bounce back out as nestle among the granite. The ninth and eighteenth play parallel to each other but offer different experiences. The 365-yard ninth plays uphill to a large green, which is connected to the eighteenth green. Conversely, the approach at eighteen is downhill. But with the large undulating green tucked in below the modest hilltop clubhouse, this is as dramatic a finishing hole as the first is an opening hole. A cart is provided to take you and your clubs up the steep incline to the clubhouse. There's a small snack bar, no driving range, no club pro, and they don't have a liquor license. Belgrade Lakes is pure golf.

COURSES NEARBY: Capitol City, Kennebec Heights, Natanis, Pine Ridge, Sandy River, Waterville, Western View

BETHEL INN & COUNTRY CLUB

BOX 49
ON THE COMMON
BETHEL
207-824-2175
WEB: www.bethelinn.com
REGION: Western Lakes and Mountains
MAP: 10
ESTABLISHED: 1913
NUMBER OF HOLES: 18
COURSE LENGTH/PAR: Back: 6,663/72   **Middle:** 6,330/72   **Front:** 5,280/72
COURSE RATING/SLOPE: Back: 72.3/133 **Middle:** 70.6/130   **Front:** 71.4/129
HEAD PROFESSIONAL: Yes
COURSE ARCHITECT: Geoffrey Cornish
GOLF FACILITIES: Full pro shop, driving range, practice green, club rental, club repair, club storage, cart rental, pull-cart rental, instruction, golf school, restaurant, lounge, accommodations
TEE TIMES: Necessary
RANGER: Yes
TEE-OFF INTERVAL TIME: 10 minutes

TIME TO PLAY 18 HOLES: 4 hours, 30 minutes
EARLIEST TEE-OFF: 7a.m.
GREEN FEES: Weekend (18): $$$$ **Weekday (18):** $$$$
PAYMENT: MasterCard, Visa, American Express
SEASON: May 1 through October 26
LOCAL CHAMBER OF COMMERCE: Bethel Area, 207-824-2282
LOCAL ATTRACTIONS: Bethel, Sunday River, White Mountain National Forest, hiking
DIRECTIONS: Take the Maine Turnpike to Exit 11. Follow Route 26 north to Bethel. At the top of Main Street, turn left onto Broad Street and look for a large yellow building.
COURSE DESCRIPTION: The Bethel Inn was originally built to house the upscale patients—doctors, lawyers, corporate executives—of Dr. John Gehring's renowned clinic for the "mentally malaised." It was these patients who, as part of their therapy, picked rocks, cleared land, and helped build the original nine-hole layout. The inn, vastly expanded and modernized, now sports an 18-hole design (which incorporates 7 of the original holes) by Geoffrey Cornish. The clinic no longer exists, but the therapeutic properties of the fresh mountain air at this year-round resort located in the foothills of the White Mountains are undeniable. Rated among the top resort courses in the Northeast, the track is scenic and a good test. The tee shot on the 144-yard par-3 third, for example, needs to clear the picturesque 150-year-old Mill Brook Dam to reach the double green (shared with the 533-yard par-5 eighth) on the far side. The short, 292-yard, par-4 ninth is complicated by a sharp back-to-front-sloping green. The elevated green at the 190-yard twelfth is small and tough to hit. And the approach at the 433-yard par-4 fifteenth, although downhill, must clear a small creek that fronts the green. Tree-lined, this course is at its visual glory at the height of leaf season in October.
COURSES NEARBY: Lake Kezar, Oakdale

BIDDEFORD-SACO GOLF CLUB
101 OLD ORCHARD ROAD
SACO
207-282-5883
REGION: Southern Coast
MAP: 3
ESTABLISHED: 1929
NUMBER OF HOLES: 18
COURSE LENGTH/PAR: Back: 6,196/71   **Middle:** 5,744/71   **Front:** 5,433/72
COURSE RATING/SLOPE: Back: 69.6/123 **Middle:** 68.6/114   **Front:** 71.4/117
HEAD PROFESSIONAL: Yes
COURSE ARCHITECT: Donald Ross, Cornish & Silva
GOLF FACILITIES: Full pro shop, driving range, practice green, practice bunker, club rental, club repair, club storage, cart rental, pull-cart rental, instruction,

locker room, showers, restaurant, lounge

Tee Times: Recommended

How Long in Advance: 3 days

Ranger: Yes

Tee-Off Interval Time: 8 minutes

Time to Play 18 Holes: 4 hours, 30 minutes

Earliest Tee-Off: 6 a.m.

Green Fees: Weekend (18): $$$ **Weekday (18): $$$**

Payment: MasterCard, Visa, American Express

Season: April 1 through November 14

Local Chamber of Commerce: Biddeford-Saco, 207-282-1567

Local Attractions: Old Orchard Beach and area beaches; 20 minutes to Portland

Directions: From the Maine Turnpike (I-95) take Exit 5. In 2½ miles turn right onto Old Orchard Road. The course is ½ mile ahead on your left.

Course Description: In 1922 Donald Ross designed 18 holes for the membership at Biddeford-Saco Country Club, but only 9 were built. It would be another 65 years before the second nine—with some variations by the firm of Cornish & Silva—would be opened. The result is considered one of the top courses in southern Maine, more difficult than the scorecard appears but still very fair. The green at the 391-yard par-4 fifth is classic Donald Ross. With lots of breaks, locals says it's almost better to miss your approach and chip on rather than end up on the wrong part of the green. Holes nine through eleven constitute Biddeford-Saco's version of Augusta National's Amen Corner. The relatively tame 145-yard tenth is sandwiched between the 425-yard ninth and 438-yard eleventh, the number one and two handicap holes, respectively. The 316-yard par-4 fourteenth doglegs left along a marsh that runs up left of the green. A pond guards the right side. If nothing else, it makes for one beautiful golf hole. Your green fee makes you a member for the day.

Courses Nearby: Cape Arundel, Dunegrass, Dutch Elm, Nonesuch River, Old Orchard Beach, Pleasant Hill, Sanford, Webhannet, Willowdale

Birch Point Golf Club

Birch Point Road

St. David

207-895-6957

Region: Aroostook

Map: 68

Established: 1961

Number of Holes: 9

Course Length/Par: Back: 5,910/70   **Middle:** 5,520/70   **Front:** 5,130/72

Course Rating/Slope: Back: NA   **Middle:** NA   **Front:** NA

Head Professional: Yes

COURSE ARCHITECT: Ben Gray

GOLF FACILITIES: Full pro shop, driving range, practice green, club rental, club repair, club storage, cart rental, pull-cart rental, instruction, locker room, showers, restaurant, lounge

TEE TIMES: Not necessary

RANGER: No

TIME TO PLAY 18 HOLES: 4 hours

EARLIEST TEE-OFF: Daybreak

GREEN FEES: Weekend (18): $ Weekday (18): $

PAYMENT: MasterCard, Visa

SEASON: May through September

LOCAL CHAMBER OF COMMERCE: Greater Fort Kent Area, 207-834-5354

LOCAL ATTRACTIONS: Long Lake, St. John River

DIRECTIONS: From Caribou take Route 161 North to Route 162. Turn right onto Route 162 to St. Agatha, then right onto Cleveland Avenue. After approximately 3 miles turn right onto Fongemie Farm Road and right again onto Lake Road. It's 1 mile to Birch Point Road.

COURSE DESCRIPTION: Located on Long Lake in the far reaches of northern Maine, Birch Point primarily plays host to local papermill workers. This is a short, wide-open layout with small greens. A brook runs though five holes, and a pond guards the green on the 290-yard par-4 fourth, so there is trouble to be had. As you might expect, there's a very casual, friendly atmosphere with a very accommodating log clubhouse.

COURSES NEARBY: Fort Kent

BLINK BONNIE GOLF CLUB

ROUTE 185

SORRENTO

207-422-3930

REGION: Acadia/Down East

MAP: 16

ESTABLISHED: 1916

NUMBER OF HOLES: 9

COURSE LENGTH/PAR: Back: 5,680/72   **Front:** 5,280/70

COURSE RATING/SLOPE: Back: 65.0/112 **Front:** NA

HEAD PROFESSIONAL: No

GOLF FACILITIES: Club rental, pull-cart rental

TEE TIMES: Not necessary

RANGER: No

TIME TO PLAY 18 HOLES: 3 hours, 30 minutes

EARLIEST TEE-OFF: 8 a.m.

GREEN FEES: Weekend (18): $$ Weekday (18): $

PAYMENT: Cash only

SEASON: May 1 through September 30

LOCAL CHAMBER OF COMMERCE: Ellsworth Area, 207-667-5584

LOCAL ATTRACTIONS: Mount Desert Island, Schoodic Peninsula

DIRECTIONS: From Ellsworth take Route 1 East to Route 185. In 2 miles look for the course on your left.

COURSE DESCRIPTION: A nine-hole layout established in 1916 and as pretty as its name implies. Off the beaten path, it qualifies as one of Maine's hidden gems. Located on Flanders Bay (east of Mount Desert Island), it has four holes that border the ocean—close enough that it comes into play. It's an open layout with bunkers guarding its velvet bentgrass greens. They hold well but, admittedly, can be slow. The fairways on the two par-5s, the 510-yard fourth and 490-yard fifth, actually cross each other. The view from the sixth green looks out over the bay to Mount Desert Island and nearby Winter Harbor. A real treat for the adventurous.

COURSES NEARBY: Grindstone Neck, White Birches

BOOTHBAY COUNTRY CLUB

COUNTRY CLUB ROAD

BOOTHBAY

207-633-6085

WEB: www.boothbaycountryclub.com

REGION: Mid-Coast Region

MAP: 7

ESTABLISHED: 1921

NUMBER OF HOLES: 9 (expanding to 18 in 2000)

COURSE LENGTH/PAR: Back: 5,382/70   **Front:** 4,916/70

COURSE RATING/SLOPE: Back: 66.1/118 **Front:** 67.2/115

HEAD PROFESSIONAL: Yes

COURSE ARCHITECT: Stiles & Van Kleek

GOLF FACILITIES: Full pro shop, driving range, practice green, club rental, club repair, cart rental, pull-cart rental, instruction, snack bar, lounge

TEE TIMES: Recommended

RANGER: Yes

TEE-OFF INTERVAL TIME: 8 minutes

TIME TO PLAY 18 HOLES: 4 hours, 15 minutes

EARLIEST TEE-OFF: 7 a.m.

GREEN FEES: Weekend (18): $$ **Weekday (18): $$**

PAYMENT: All major credit cards

SEASON: Mid-April through October 31

LOCAL CHAMBER OF COMMERCE: Boothbay Harbor Region, 207-633-2353

LOCAL ATTRACTIONS: Windjammer Days, whale-watching, boat excursions, shopping

DIRECTIONS: From Route 1 take Route 27 to Boothbay. In about 8 miles look for Country Club Road on left. Course 1/4 mile on right.

COURSE DESCRIPTION: A classic nine-hole layout located near one of Maine's premier vacation destinations. The first and second holes set the tone on this short links-style course. The opening hole is a 346-yard downhill dogleg right that plays back uphill to an elevated green tucked hard against a grassy bank with woods beyond. At 176 yards, the par-3 second is equally picturesque. An elevated tee leads to a large, undulating green with large pines lining both sides. Changes are in store, with a new nine being built and due to open in 2000. The new holes will be incorporated into the original layout and promise to maintain the vintage character of this Stiles and Van Kleek design.

COURSES NEARBY: Bath, Wawenock

BRIDGTON HIGHLANDS COUNTRY CLUB

HIGHLAND ROAD
BRIDGTON
207-647-3491
REGION: Western Lakes and Mountains
MAP: 31
ESTABLISHED: 1926
NUMBER OF HOLES: 18
COURSE LENGTH/PAR: Back: 6,059/72   **Middle:** 5,820/72   **Front:** 5,093/72
COURSE RATING/SLOPE: Back: 70.2/126 **Middle:** 69.3/123 **Front:** 67.0/118
HEAD PROFESSIONAL: Yes
COURSE ARCHITECT: Ralph Barton (O9); Fred Ryan, Cornish & Silva (A9)
GOLF FACILITIES: Full pro shop, practice green, club rental, club repair, cart rental, pull-cart rental, instruction, locker room, snack bar, lounge
TEE TIMES: Recommended
HOW LONG IN ADVANCE: 3 days
RANGER: Yes
TEE-OFF INTERVAL TIME: 8 minutes
TIME TO PLAY 18 HOLES: 4 hours, 15 minutes
EARLIEST TEE-OFF: 7:00 a.m.
GREEN FEES: Weekend (18): $$ **Weekday (18): $$**
PAYMENT: MasterCard, Visa, Discover
SEASON: April 15 through October 31
LOCAL CHAMBER OF COMMERCE: Bridgton Lakes Region, 207-647-3472
LOCAL ATTRACTIONS: Sebago Lake, boating, fishing
DIRECTIONS: Take Route 302 to Bridgton. Turn right onto Highland Road at Highland Lake Beach. In two miles look for the course on your right.
COURSE DESCRIPTION: The original nine was designed by Ralph Barton, who

assisted C. B. Macdonald in the design of Yale Golf Club (Connecticut) and Mid Ocean Club (Bermuda). Set atop a ridge with stunning views of Shawnee Peak Ski Area and the White Mountains to the west, the current layout incorporates nine new holes that cut through thick woods. Bridgton Highlands features one of the toughest opening holes in the state. Appropriately named Tough Start, the 440-yard par-4 first has trees and a few fairway bunkers down the left side, and out of bounds to the right. Although straightaway, it's a tight opening for the first shot of a round. The wetland hazard traversing the 376-yard par-4 third is typical of the new holes and requires accuracy and good course management. Many locals opt to lay up in front of the hazard leaving a long approach—or another lay-up—to a small green with more water in front. Stonework around some of the new tee boxes add to the course's overall beauty which culminates on your approach to the eighteenth green, where the John Calvin Stevens–designed clubhouse provides a pretty backdrop.

COURSES NEARBY: Allen Mountain, Frye Island, Lake Kezar, Naples, Point Sebago

BRUNSWICK GOLF CLUB

RIVER ROAD
BRUNSWICK
207-725-8224
REGION: Mid-Coast Region
MAP: 6
ESTABLISHED: 1901
NUMBER OF HOLES: 18
COURSE LENGTH/PAR: Back: 6,609/72   **Middle:** 6,251/72   **Front:** 5,772/74
COURSE RATING/SLOPE: Back: 71.0/128 **Middle:** 69.5/123   **Front:** 71.6/123
HEAD PROFESSIONAL: Yes
COURSE ARCHITECT: Stiles & Van Kleek; Geoffrey Cornish (A9)
GOLF FACILITIES: Full pro shop, driving range, practice green, club rental, club repair, club storage, cart rental, pull-cart rental, instruction, locker room, showers, restaurant, lounge
TEE TIMES: Recommended
HOW LONG IN ADVANCE: 3 days
RANGER: Yes
TEE-OFF INTERVAL TIME: 9 minutes
TIME TO PLAY 18 HOLES: 4 hours, 15 minutes
EARLIEST TEE-OFF: 7:30 a.m.
**GREEN FEES: Weekend (18): $$$ Weekday (18): $$$
PAYMENT: MasterCard, Visa
SEASON: April 1 through November 15
LOCAL CHAMBER OF COMMERCE: Bath-Brunswick Region, 207-725-8797
LOCAL ATTRACTIONS: Bowdoin College, Brunswick Naval Air Station
DIRECTIONS: Take Exit 22 off I-95, then take Route 1 North to River Road.

Turn left onto River Road; it's 1 mile to the club.

COURSE DESCRIPTION: The original nine holes were built here at the turn of the century by Bowdoin College students. It wasn't until the 1920s that architects Stiles & Van Kleek were enlisted to remodel and expand on this layout. In 1970 Geoffrey Cornish added nine new holes. The result is two distinct loops, the front nine being the newer of the two. A challenging layout, this 6,251-yard track's front nine features consecutive par-5s, followed by consecutive par-3s. It's the latter that tend to receive the most attention on this course. The 175-yard fourth requires a drive over water to a green guarded by a bunker left. Miss it to the right and you're sure to catch the steep bank that falls into the pond. The fifth heads back over the water hazard to a very small green just 110 yards away. The older back nine is shorter, has its own share of challenges, and is every bit as enjoyable. Brunswick played host to the 1998 Maine Amateur.

COURSES NEARBY: Bath, Freeport, Mere Creek, Shore Acres

BUCKSPORT GOLF COURSE
ROUTE 46
BUCKSPORT
207-469-7612

REGION: Acadia/Down East

MAP: 23

ESTABLISHED: 1969

NUMBER OF HOLES: 9

COURSE LENGTH/PAR: Back: 6,749/72   **Front:** 5,578/72

COURSE RATING/SLOPE: Back: 70.6/117 **Front:** 72.2/115

HEAD PROFESSIONAL: Yes

COURSE ARCHITECT: Philip Wogan

GOLF FACILITIES: Full pro shop, driving range, practice green, club rental, club repair, club storage, cart rental, pull-cart rental, instruction, locker room, showers, snack bar, lounge

TEE TIMES: Not necessary

RANGER: No

TIME TO PLAY 18 HOLES: 4 hours, 30 minutes

EARLIEST TEE-OFF: 7 a.m.

GREEN FEES: Weekend (18): $$ Weekday (18): $$

PAYMENT: MasterCard, Visa

SEASON: April through September

LOCAL CHAMBER OF COMMERCE: Bucksport Bay Area, 207-469-6818

LOCAL ATTRACTIONS: Fort Knox, Penobscot River

DIRECTIONS: Take Route 1 to Bucksport, then turn left onto Route 46. The course is 2 to 3 miles ahead on your right.

COURSE DESCRIPTION: Bucksport ranks as the longest nine-hole layout in the state. In fact, the club has probably devoted more acreage to 9 holes than most larger clubs do to 18. Long is certainly the name of the game here. A wide-open layout, the course is characterized by hills and valleys. The 454-yard par-4 second features a blind tee shot into a huge swale. At best you're faced with a long approach into the large green, which is guarded by water in front. Holes five and six (a 502-yard par-5 and 188-yard par-3, respectively) slope right to left toward the bordering Naramissic River. Both are uphill, so they tend to play longer than the scorecard indicates.

COURSES NEARBY: Castine, Lucerne-in-Maine, Searsport Pines, Streamside

CAPE ARUNDEL GOLF CLUB
19 RIVER ROAD
KENNEBUNKPORT
207-967-3494
REGION: Southern Coast
MAP: 3
ESTABLISHED: 1897
NUMBER OF HOLES: 18
COURSE LENGTH/PAR: Back: 5,869/69   **Front:** 5,134/70
COURSE RATING/SLOPE: Back: 67.0/117 **Front:** 68.6/106
HEAD PROFESSIONAL: Yes
COURSE ARCHITECT: Walter Travis
GOLF FACILITIES: Full pro shop, practice green, club rental, club repair, club storage, cart rental, pull-cart rental, instruction, locker room, showers
TEE TIMES: Necessary
HOW LONG IN ADVANCE: 24 hours only
RANGER: Yes
TEE-OFF INTERVAL TIME: 12 minutes
TIME TO PLAY 18 HOLES: Under 4 hours
EARLIEST TEE-OFF: 6:30 a.m.
GREEN FEES: Weekend (18): $$$ Weekday (18): $$$
PAYMENT: Cash only
SEASON: Mid-April through mid-November
LOCAL CHAMBER OF COMMERCE: Kennebunk-Kennebunkport, 207-967-0857
LOCAL ATTRACTIONS: Area beaches, shopping, Walker Point
DIRECTIONS: Take Exit 2 off the Maine Turnpike (I-95). Turn left onto Route 109, then
left again onto Route 1, which you follow for 2 miles to Route 9 East. Take Route 9 about 6 miles through Kennebunkport. At the top of the hill, take a left onto Main Street. In 1 mile bear left at a fork; the course is on your left.
COURSE DESCRIPTION: Designed by Walter Travis, winner of several U.S. Amateur titles, Cape Arundel is the home course of former president George Bush when in residence at Walker Point. Bush's grandfather George Herbert Walker, a

former club president, was founder of the Walker Cup (amateur golf's version of the Ryder Cup). His father, Prescott Bush, was a past president of the USGA and for a time shared the course record currently held by Fred Couples at 62. A fairly open layout with sloping greens, Cape Arundel favors the left-to-right player. At this vintage links-style course most holes run in close proximity to each other and feature mounds in the fairways and around the greens that often make for awkward chip shots. One of Arundel's classic holes is the 165-yard thirteenth. A river runs down in front of the green, which sits on a peninsula with bunkers to the right. There is a great deal of history here. The layout is virtually the same as designed and is pleasantly understated despite its celebrity status.

COURSES NEARBY: Biddeford-Saco, Dunegrass, Dutch Elm, Old Orchard Beach, Sanford, Webhannet

CAPE NEDDICK COUNTRY CLUB
SHORE ROAD
CAPE NEDDICK 03092
207-361-2011
WEB: www.capeneddickgolf.com
REGION: Southern Coast
MAP: 1
ESTABLISHED: 1902
NUMBER OF HOLES: 18
COURSE LENGTH/PAR: Back: 6,052/70   **Middle:** 5,682/70   **Front:** 4,866/70
COURSE RATING/SLOPE: Back: 68.4/112 **Middle:** 66.6/110   **Front:** 67.8/114
HEAD PROFESSIONAL: Yes
COURSE ARCHITECT: Donald Ross (O9), Brian Silva (A9)
GOLF FACILITIES: Full pro shop, driving range, practice green, club rental, club storage, cart rental, pull-cart rental, instruction, locker room, showers, restaurant, lounge
TEE TIMES: Necessary
HOW LONG IN ADVANCE: 1 day
RANGER: Yes
TEE-OFF INTERVAL TIME: 8 minutes
TIME TO PLAY 18 HOLES: 4 hours, 15 minutes
EARLIEST TEE-OFF: 7 a.m.
GREEN FEES: Weekend (18): $$$$ Weekday (18): $$$$
PAYMENT: MasterCard, Visa
SEASON: April 1 through November 1
LOCAL CHAMBER OF COMMERCE: Ogunquit, 207-646-2939
LOCAL ATTRACTIONS: Ogunquit, area beaches
DIRECTIONS: Take the Maine Turnpike (I-95) to the York Exit (Exit 4). Turn right (north) off the ramp onto Route 1 and drive approximately 3⅓ miles to River

Road. Turn right and follow River Road approximately 1 mile to Shore Road. Take a left; the club is about 3 miles ahead on your left.

COURSE DESCRIPTION: This semiprivate resort course caters primarily to its members but offers limited public access. In season only, guests staying at member hotel or motels are permitted to use the club on a space-available basis. During the "shoulder" seasons, it is open to public play on a space-available basis. A golf course has existed here since 1902, when six holes were laid out for use by guests of the nearby Cliff House hotel. In 1920 Donald Ross was hired to remodel and expand the course into a full 18 holes. As happened with so many courses at the time, the back nine was abandoned during World War II, and and the club operated as a nine-hole course for more than 50 years. In 1996 the club explored the restoration of the abandoned holes, but because much of the land was on what today is defined as wetlands, restoration was not feasible. Instead management engaged Brian Silva, an avid student of Donald Ross, to add nine new holes. Rather than have an old nine and a new nine, the new layout incorporates the old holes. Silva's assignment was to "mimic the old holes to reflect the Donald Ross feel." His creation opened in summer 1999; early indications are that it achieves that goal.

COURSES NEARBY: Highland Links, The Ledges, Links at Outlook

CAPITOL CITY GOLF COURSE
OLD BELGRADE ROAD
AUGUSTA
207-623-0504
REGION: Kennebec/Moose River Region
MAP: 12
ESTABLISHED: 1992
NUMBER OF HOLES: 18
COURSE LENGTH/PAR: Back: 3,874/63   **Front:** 3,381/63
COURSE RATING/SLOPE: Back: NA   **Front:** NA
HEAD PROFESSIONAL: Yes
COURSE ARCHITECT: Richard Violette
GOLF FACILITIES: Full pro shop, driving range, practice green, club rental, club repair, cart rental, pull-cart rental, instruction, snack bar
TEE TIMES: Not necessary
RANGER: No
TIME TO PLAY 18 HOLES: 3 hours
EARLIEST TEE-OFF: 7 a.m.
GREEN FEES: Weekend (18): $ Weekday (18): $
PAYMENT: MasterCard, Visa
SEASON: May through September
LOCAL CHAMBER OF COMMERCE: Kennebec Valley, 207-623-4559
LOCAL ATTRACTIONS: Greater Augusta area, lakes

DIRECTIONS: Take Route 27 toward Belgrade. The course is about 3½ miles ahead on your right.

COURSE DESCRIPTION: The front nine here was built in 1992 as a par-3 course that measures 1,084 yards; holes range from 93 to 162 yards. The newer back nine is a full 2,790-yard par-36 layout and features a number of blind shots. Built on former farmland, it is a wide open layout with good-size greens. Back-to-back par-5s at number thirteen (a 479-yard dogleg left) and the 520-yard fourteenth present a good challenge. A new irrigation pond was built in 1998. The course is located on the outskirts of Maine's capital city, Augusta.

COURSES NEARBY: Belgrade Lakes, Kennebec Heights, Natanis, Western View

CARIBOU COUNTRY CLUB
SWEDEN ROAD
CARIBOU
207-493-3933
REGION: Aroostook
MAP: 65
ESTABLISHED: 1971
NUMBER OF HOLES: 9
COURSE LENGTH/PAR: Back: 6,433/72   **Front:** 5,631/72
COURSE RATING/SLOPE: Back: 69.6/116 **Front:** NA
HEAD PROFESSIONAL: Yes
COURSE ARCHITECT: Ben Gray
GOLF FACILITIES: Full pro shop, driving range, practice green, club rental, club repair, cart rental, pull-cart rental, instruction, locker room, showers, snack bar, lounge
TEE TIMES: Not necessary
RANGER: No
TIME TO PLAY 18 HOLES: 4 hours
EARLIEST TEE-OFF: 7 a.m.
GREEN FEES: Weekend (18): $ Weekday (18): $
PAYMENT: MasterCard, Visa
SEASON: May 1 through October 15
LOCAL CHAMBER OF COMMERCE: Caribou, 800-722-7648
LOCAL ATTRACTIONS: Hiking, bog walks
DIRECTIONS: The course is found on Route 161 about 2 miles from its junction with Route 228, on your right.
COURSE DESCRIPTION: Best known in winter as a snowmobiler's heaven, the town of Caribou (the fifth snowiest city in the United States) sports a charming nine-hole track. Former farmland sets the stage for this 6,433-yard Ben Gray design. Most memorable are the long par-5s, especially number two. At 515 yards, bunkers play havoc with your tee shot, and the prevailing wind makes it seem

even longer. The 340-yard par-4 sixth is the prettiest on the course, playing over a gully to a slightly elevated green. Though fairly wide open, there are plenty of well-placed bunkers—38 in all—which were recently refilled with fine white sand.

Courses Nearby: Aroostook Valley, Limestone, Mars Hill, Presque Isle

Carmel Valley Golf Links

Main Road
Carmel
207-848-2582
Region: Katahdin/Moosehead Region
Map: 22
Established: 1971
Number of Holes: 9
Course Length/Par: Back: 2,714/54   **Middle:** 2,518/54   **Front:** 2,208/54
Course Rating/Slope: Back: NA   **Middle:** NA   **Front:** NA
Head Professional: No
Course Architect: Ted Johns
Golf Facilities: Full pro shop, practice green, club rental, pull-cart rental, instruction, snack bar, lounge
Tee Times: Not necessary
Ranger: No
Time to Play 18 Holes: 2 hours, 20 minutes
Earliest Tee-Off: 6 a.m.
Green Fees: Weekend (18): $ Weekday (18): $
Payment: Cash only
Season: April through November 1
Local Chamber of Commerce: Bangor Region, 207-947-0307
Local Attractions: Greater Bangor area
Directions: From Exit 43 off I-95 take Route 69 West to Carmel village. Head west on Route 2 for about 1/3 mile.

Course Description: A family-oriented executive course that's a good test for all levels "including the guys who think they're good." The course record is an even par 54. All holes have been given names based on their characteristics. A favorite is Hit and Take Six, a 133-yarder with a severely sloped green protected by ponds just off the tee and along the right side. An annual junior tournament—for which the parents are caddies—is held each summer and is open to all ages and ability levels.

Courses Nearby: Bangor Municipal, Hermon Meadows, Kenduskeag, Orchard View

CASTINE GOLF CLUB

BATTLE AVENUE
CASTINE
207-326-8844
REGION: Acadia/Down East
MAP: 15
ESTABLISHED: 1897
NUMBER OF HOLES: 9
COURSE LENGTH/PAR: Back: 5,954/70   **Front:** 5,458/72
COURSE RATING/SLOPE: Back: 68.1/116 **Front:** 71.4/122
HEAD PROFESSIONAL: Yes
COURSE ARCHITECT: Willie Park Jr.
GOLF FACILITIES: Full pro shop, practice green, club rental, cart rental, pull-cart rental, instruction
TEE TIMES: Not necessary
RANGER: No
TIME TO PLAY 18 HOLES: 4 hours, 15 minutes
EARLIEST TEE-OFF: 8 a.m.
GREEN FEES: Weekend (18): $$ **Weekday (18): $$**
PAYMENT: Cash only
SEASON: May 15 through October 15
LOCAL CHAMBER OF COMMERCE: Ellsworth Area, 207-667-5584
LOCAL ATTRACTIONS: Fort George, Maine Maritime Academy, historic sites
DIRECTIONS: From Bucksport take Route 175 to Route 166 into Castine. The course is on your right as you enter town.
COURSE DESCRIPTION: When it was formed in 1897, the club featured a small member-designed course that meandered through various backyards and even through the earthworks of an 18th-century British fort. In 1921 former British Open champion (1887 and 1889) Willie Park Jr. was engaged to draw up the current layout, which covers much of the same ground (less the fort). Maintained to the original design—the blueprints of which can be viewed on request—the course is open but deceiving. Bumps, bunkers, and blind shots will challenge all levels. The 397-yard third features a large grass pit coming in from the right about 190 yards out; the fairway slopes right to left—toward the woods. The sixth hole is all of 344 yards, but the steeply uphill approach is blind and the tricky horseshoe-shaped green is guarded on either side by large inviting bunkers. (The view from this green of the Bagaduce River is the best on the course.) The 465-yard par-5 seventh—which some say is reminiscent of Park's work at Maidstone Club in Easthampton, New York—features a unique green that tiers right to left. The clubhouse is available for members only, but the historic town of Castine is worth the visit.
COURSES NEARBY: Bucksport, Island

CAUSEWAY GOLF CLUB

FERNALD POINT ROAD
SOUTHWEST HARBOR
207-244-3780
REGION: Acadia/Down East
MAP: 16
ESTABLISHED: 1920
NUMBER OF HOLES: 9
COURSE LENGTH/PAR: Back: 4,718/65   **Front:** 4,360/67
COURSE RATING/SLOPE: BACK: 60.8/90   **FRONT:** NA
HEAD PROFESSIONAL: Yes
COURSE ARCHITECT: NA
GOLF FACILITIES: Full pro shop, practice green, club rental, club repair, club storage, cart rental, pull-cart rental, instruction, snack bar
TEE TIMES: Not necessary
RANGER: No
TIME TO PLAY 18 HOLES: 3 hours
EARLIEST TEE-OFF: 7 a.m.
GREEN FEES: Weekend (18): $$$ **Weekday (18): $$$**
PAYMENT: MasterCard, Visa
SEASON: May 1 through mid-October
LOCAL CHAMBER OF COMMERCE: Southwest Harbor–Tremont, 207-244-9264
LOCAL ATTRACTIONS: Acadia National Park, Somes Sound, boat excursions, hiking
DIRECTIONS: Take Route 102 toward Southwest Harbor. Turn left onto Fernald Point Road just before entering town.
COURSE DESCRIPTION: This is Mount Desert Island's only nine-hole track. Built in the early 1930s, it is, for the most part, a short, open layout ideal for beginners but fun for all levels. Holes are straightaway with few hazards. The lone exception would be the 228-yard par-3 seventh, which requires that you negotiate Norwood Cove for a good portion of its length. A large green awaits, but the slope leading up to it will cause problems for a short drive. The small clubhouse has few facilities. (Lobster-boat enthusiasts will enjoy the views from nearby Bass Harbor and Bernard.)
COURSES NEARBY: Bar Harbor, Kebo Valley Club, Northeast Harbor

CEDAR SPRINGS GOLF COURSE

BOG ROAD
ALBION
207-437-2073
REGION: Kennebec/Moose River Region
MAP: 21

ESTABLISHED: 1997

NUMBER OF HOLES: 9

COURSE LENGTH/PAR: Back: 6,120/71   **Middle:** 5,790/71   **Front:** 5,350/71

COURSE RATING/SLOPE: Back: NA   **Middle:** 65.6/109   **Front:** NA

HEAD PROFESSIONAL: No

COURSE ARCHITECT: Greg and Tim Theriault

GOLF FACILITIES: Practice green, club rental, cart rental, pull-cart rental, snack bar

TEE TIMES: Not necessary

RANGER: Yes

TIME TO PLAY 18 HOLES: 4 hours

EARLIEST TEE-OFF: 6 a.m.

GREEN FEES: Weekend (18): $ Weekday (18): $

PAYMENT: MasterCard, Visa

SEASON: Mid-April through October 31

LOCAL CHAMBER OF COMMERCE: Mid-Maine, 207-873-3315 or 3316

LOCAL ATTRACTIONS: Lakes, fishing

DIRECTIONS: The course is 3/4 mile north of Albion. From Route 37 turn left onto Bog Road (by a church); it will be 1,500 feet ahead on your right.

COURSE DESCRIPTION: Locally designed and built, Cedar Springs (just 20 minutes east of Waterville) offers a unique set of challenges. Starting with the narrow 300-yard par-4 first, which features a blind, uphill tee shot toward a pond that encroaches from the right about 160 yards out, you'll work for par on most holes. The 405-yard dogleg left fourth, for example, plays to a small target protected by a berm in front that can either trap your approach shot short or kick your ball off the back of the green. The par-4 fifth, at just 269 yards, would seem simple enough, except for a large pine tree guarding the very middle of its narrow fairway. There is a small pro shop with limited facilities.

COURSES NEARBY: Lakeview, Natanis, Pine Ridge, Waterville

COBBOSSEE COLONY GOLF COURSE

COBBOSSEECONTEE ROAD
MONMOUTH
207- 268-4182

REGION: Kennebec/Moose River Region

MAP: 12

ESTABLISHED: 1926

NUMBER OF HOLES: 9

COURSE LENGTH/PAR: Back: 4,758/68   **Front:** 4,358/72

COURSE RATING/SLOPE: Back: 63.0/108   **Front:** 64.3/104

HEAD PROFESSIONAL: Yes

COURSE ARCHITECT: Royal and Lee Cottrell

GOLF FACILITIES: Driving range, practice green, practice bunker, club rental, club repair, cart rental, pull-cart rental, instruction, snack bar

TEE TIMES: Not necessary

RANGER: Yes

TIME TO PLAY 18 HOLES: 3 hours, 30 minutes

EARLIEST TEE-OFF: 6 a.m.

GREEN FEES: Weekend (18): $ Weekday (18): $

PAYMENT: MasterCard, Visa

SEASON: Mid-April till snow

LOCAL CHAMBER OF COMMERCE: Kennebec Valley, 207-623-4559

LOCAL ATTRACTIONS: Cobbossee Lake, Augusta

DIRECTIONS: From Gardiner take Route 126 toward Litchfield. Take a right at Bachelor Tavern, then another right onto Hardscrabble Road. The course is 1 1/2 miles ahead at the south end of Cobbossee Lake.

COURSE DESCRIPTION: A short layout designed as part of a summer resort colony near the southern tip of Cobbossee Lake, this nine-hole layout is open with few hazards but offers its share of challenges just the same. The 515-yard par-5 first hole, for example, is a dogleg right with woods along the right side. For most it requires three good shots to reach the small green. And small greens are the norm here. An easy-walking course with a friendly atmosphere, Cobbossee Colony is popular with beginners and seniors alike.

COURSES NEARBY: Kennebec Heights, The Meadows, Springbrook, Western View

COUNTRY VIEW GOLF CLUB

ROUTE 7

BROOKS

207-722-3161

REGION: Mid-Coast Region

MAP: 22

ESTABLISHED: 1964

NUMBER OF HOLES: 9

COURSE LENGTH/PAR: Back: 5,900/72   **Front:** 4,960/72

COURSE RATING/SLOPE: Back: 68.0/113   **Front:** NA

HEAD PROFESSIONAL: Yes

COURSE ARCHITECT: Ralph Brown

GOLF FACILITIES: Full pro shop, driving range, practice green, club rental, cart rental, pull-cart rental, instruction, snack bar

TEE TIMES: Not necessary

RANGER: Yes

TIME TO PLAY 18 HOLES: 4 hours, 30 minutes

EARLIEST TEE-OFF: 6 a.m.

GREEN FEES: Weekend (18): $ Weekday (18): $

PAYMENT: Cash only

SEASON: April 15 through October 31

LOCAL CHAMBER OF COMMERCE: Belfast Area, 207-338-5900

LOCAL ATTRACTIONS: Swan Lake

DIRECTIONS: The course is 1½ miles north of Brooks village on Route 7.

COURSE DESCRIPTION: Country View is a beautiful nine-hole layout that plays around the top of a hill amid rolling farmland. One of central Maine's most scenic courses, it features a different view on every hole, including—on a clear day—the White Mountains to the west and the Camden Hills and even Cadillac Mountain to the south and east. There is some sand, some water, and a lot of trees. Its hillside location makes for some interesting uphill and downhill lies as well as the occasional blind shot. Classic among these is the tee shot on the 340-yard par-4 seventh, where a 24-foot periscope has been erected to let you see if the green is clear. The course is well maintained and the atmosphere very friendly.

COURSES NEARBY: Lakeview, Northport, Searsport Pines, Streamside

DEXTER MUNICIPAL GOLF CLUB
35 SUNRISE AVENUE
DEXTER
207-924-6477

REGION: Katahdin/Moosehead Region

MAP: 32

ESTABLISHED: 1968

NUMBER OF HOLES: 9

COURSE LENGTH/PAR: Back: 5,241/70   **Front:** 4,784/70

COURSE RATING/SLOPE: Back: 65.7/115   **Front:** NA

HEAD PROFESSIONAL: Yes

COURSE ARCHITECT: Bill Nadeau

GOLF FACILITIES: Full pro shop, driving range, practice green, practice bunker, club rental, club repair, club storage, cart rental, pull-cart rental, instruction, snack bar, lounge

TEE TIMES: Not necessary

RANGER: Yes

TIME TO PLAY 18 HOLES: 4 hours, 30 minutes

EARLIEST TEE-OFF: 6 a.m.

GREEN FEES: Weekend (18): $ Weekday (18): $

PAYMENT: Cash only

SEASON: April 1 through November 1

LOCAL CHAMBER OF COMMERCE: Sebasticook Valley, 207-368-4698

LOCAL ATTRACTIONS: Lakes

DIRECTIONS: Take I-95 north to Newport (Exit 39). Follow Route 7 north to Dexter.

COURSE DESCRIPTION: This nine-hole golf course was privately built in 1968

and later sold to the town of Dexter. The town is home to Dexter Shoe Company, which produces its fine line of golf shoes here. For the most part it is a fairly open layout. The par-4s are short (four of six are under 300 yards), but water comes into play on several holes, which helps make up for lack of distance. The straightway 275-yard first, for example, has a pond immediately fronting the green. The par-3s—the 173-yard fifth and the 179-yard eighth—are tough. Both have small greens, are well bunkered, and have narrow approaches.

COURSES NEARBY: Foxcroft, Palmyra, Piscataquis, Todd Valley, Whitetail

DUNEGRASS GOLF CLUB
WILD DUNES WAY
OLD ORCHARD BEACH
207-934-4513 OR 800-521-1029
WEB: www.dunegrass.com
REGION: Southern Coast
MAP: 3
ESTABLISHED: 1998
NUMBER OF HOLES: 18
COURSE LENGTH/PAR: Back: 6,515/71   **Middle:** 6,111/71   **Front:** 5,479/71
COURSE RATING/SLOPE: Back: 71.1/131 **Middle:** 68.0/123   **Front:** 65.0/115
HEAD PROFESSIONAL: Yes
COURSE ARCHITECT: Dan Maples
GOLF FACILITIES: Full pro shop, driving range, practice green, practice bunker, club rental, club repair, club storage, cart rental, pull-cart rental, instruction, locker room, showers, restaurant, lounge, banquet facility
TEE TIMES: Necessary
HOW LONG IN ADVANCE: 7 days
RANGER: Yes
TEE-OFF INTERVAL TIME: 8 minutes
TIME TO PLAY 18 HOLES: 4 hours, 30 minutes
EARLIEST TEE-OFF: 6 a.m.
GREEN FEES: Weekend (18): $$$$ **Weekday (18):** $$$$
PAYMENT: MasterCard, Visa, American Express
SEASON: April through October
LOCAL CHAMBER OF COMMERCE: Old Orchard Beach, 207-934-2500
LOCAL ATTRACTIONS: Old Orchard Beach, beaches, shopping
DIRECTIONS: From Exit 5 off the Maine Turnpike (I-95), take exit ramp 2B to Route 1 North. After 1/10 mile, take a right onto Ross Road. The course is 2 miles ahead on your right. Follow signs to the clubhouse.
COURSE DESCRIPTION: Well-known North Carolina–based designer Dan Maples laid out this 6,515-yard championship course that meanders over 320 acres of ancient sand dunes and hilly woodside near one of Maine's leading tourist desti-

nations. The course opened in 1999 to high praise from the golfing public. It will certainly will be rated one of Maine's top golf courses. With five tee boxes, the par-71 layout is, as Maples intended, playable for all levels. Starting with the first hole, for example, there is a 60-foot elevation drop between the championship and forward tees. Several yards of sandy beachfront border a pond, making any right-side green approach interesting. The seventeenth and eighteenth are two of the best finishing holes in the state. The 197-yard seventeenth plays to an island green protected in front, on the right, and in back by sand. The 548-yard par-5 eighteenth is a true three-shot hole. Distance and accuracy are necessary off the tee. Dunegrass's greens are large and undulating, and the tree-lined fairways are beautifully sculpted. Equal to the course's beauty is Dunegrass's majestic 15,000-square-foot clubhouse, which includes a large pro shop and 150-person restaurant that overlooks the eighteenth green.

COURSES NEARBY: Biddeford-Saco, Cape Arundel, Dutch Elm, Nonesuch River, Old Orchard Beach, Sable Oaks, Salmon Falls, Willowdale

DUTCH ELM GOLF CLUB

5 BRIMSTONE ROAD
ARUNDEL
207-282-9850
E-MAIL: dutchelm@cybertours.com
REGION: Southern Coast
MAP: 3
ESTABLISHED: 1965
NUMBER OF HOLES: 18
COURSE LENGTH/PAR: Back: 6,244/72   **Middle:** 5,859/72   **Front:** 5,316/73
COURSE RATING/SLOPE: Back: 71.1/125   **Middle:** 69.4/121   **Front:** 70.1/115
HEAD PROFESSIONAL: Yes
COURSE ARCHITECT: Lucien Bourque
GOLF FACILITIES: Full pro shop, driving range, practice green, club rental, club repair, cart rental, pull-cart rental, instruction, snack bar
TEE TIMES: Recommended
HOW LONG IN ADVANCE: 7 days
RANGER: Yes
TEE-OFF INTERVAL TIME: 8 minutes
TIME TO PLAY 18 HOLES: 4 hours, 15 minutes
EARLIEST TEE-OFF: 7 a.m.
GREEN FEES: Weekend (18): $$ **Weekday (18): $$**
PAYMENT: MasterCard, Visa
SEASON: April 15 through November 15
LOCAL CHAMBER OF COMMERCE: Kennebunk, 207-967-0857
LOCAL ATTRACTIONS: Kennebunkport, beaches

DIRECTIONS: At Exit 4 (Biddeford) off the Maine Turnpike (I-95), turn right onto Route 111. After about 1 mile bear left at a gas station onto New Road. Turn right onto Limerick Road. The course is on your left.

COURSE DESCRIPTION: As it says on Dutch Elm's brochure, "This par 72 layout will test your shot-making skills." Fairly tight and tree lined, this unique design features three par-5s in succession (at 13, 14, and 15) and two sets of consecutive par-3s (7 and 8; 11 and 12). Crowned greens make the bump and run your approach shot of choice. The sharp dogleg around water makes an honest par-5 out of the 431-yard fifteenth. So, too, you won't want to cut the corner on the tree-lined 342-yard seventeenth. Well maintained and a pleasant, walkable course.

COURSES NEARBY: Biddeford-Saco, Cape Arundel, Dunegrass, Nonesuch River Old Orchard Beach, Sanford, Webhannet, Willowdale

FAIRLAWN GOLF & COUNTRY CLUB
434 EMPIRE ROAD
POLAND
207-998-4277
REGION: Western Lakes and Mountains
MAP: 5
ESTABLISHED: 1961
NUMBER OF HOLES: 18
COURSE LENGTH/PAR: Back: 6,300/72   **Front:** 5,379/72
COURSE RATING/SLOPE: Back: 69.4/118 **Front:** 69.9/112
HEAD PROFESSIONAL: Yes
COURSE ARCHITECT: Chic Adams, Frank Bartasius
GOLF FACILITIES: Full pro shop, driving range, practice green, club rental, cart rental, pull-cart rental, locker room, showers, snack bar
TEE TIMES: Not necessary
RANGER: Yes
TIME TO PLAY 18 HOLES: 4 hours, 30 minutes
EARLIEST TEE-OFF: 7 a.m.
GREEN FEES: Weekend (18): $ Weekday (18): $
PAYMENT: MasterCard, Visa
SEASON: Mid-April till snow
LOCAL CHAMBER OF COMMERCE: Androscoggin County, 207-783-2249
LOCAL ATTRACTIONS: Poland Spring, Range Pond State Park
DIRECTIONS: From Exit 11 off the Maine Turnpike (I-495), follow Route 26 North toward Poland. Take a right onto Route 122, travel 1½ miles, then take a left onto Empire Road. The course is 2 miles ahead on your left.
COURSE DESCRIPTION: The "youngest" of the Poland Spring–area golf courses, Fairlawn was designed and built by Frank Bartasius, whose family still operates the course. It is noted for its large greens, which are more square than round. It

has a fairly flat layout with well-established white pines dividing its fairways. The 409-yard par-4 fourth—the number one handicap hole—plays straightaway, but trees encroach the landing area, adding to its challenge. Similarly, the par-4 tenth, an uphill 394-yard dogleg left, will require accurate club selection for your second shot. It's a blind approach that locals say requires one more club than you think you'll need. Fairlawn is a pleasantly walkable course, very well maintained, and popular with locals.

COURSES NEARBY: Point Sebago, Poland Spring, Prospect Hill, Spring Meadows, Summit

FELT BROOK GOLF CENTER

ONE MAIN ROAD
HOLDEN
207-989-3500
WEB: www.feltbrook.com
REGION: Katahdin/Moosehead Region
MAP: 23
ESTABLISHED: 1998
NUMBER OF HOLES: 9
COURSE LENGTH/PAR: Back: 4,515/66   **Front:** 3,682/68
COURSE RATING/SLOPE: Back: 62.2/99   **Front:** NA
HEAD PROFESSIONAL: Yes
COURSE ARCHITECT: NA
GOLF FACILITIES: Full pro shop, driving range, practice green, practice bunker, club rental, club repair, cart rental, pull-cart rental, instruction, restaurant, lounge, miniature golf
TEE TIMES: Recommended
HOW LONG IN ADVANCE: 7 days
RANGER: No
TEE-OFF INTERVAL TIME: 7 minutes
TIME TO PLAY 18 HOLES: 4 hours
EARLIEST TEE-OFF: 6 a.m.
GREEN FEES: Weekend (18): $ Weekday (18): $
PAYMENT: All major credit cards
SEASON: April through October
LOCAL CHAMBER OF COMMERCE: Bangor Region, 207-947-0307
LOCAL ATTRACTIONS: Greater Bangor area, Bangor Mall
DIRECTIONS: From Exit 45 off I-95 in Bangor take Route 395 toward Holden. Route 395 ends on Route 1A. Turn right onto Route 1A. The course is on your right.
COURSE DESCRIPTION: A short course located just east of Bangor, Felt Brook has just enough fairway contours, green undulations, trees, and water to make for a

good golf challenge. Holes five and six are certainly the most interesting. Number five, a 185-yard par-3, features a water encircling about 80 percent of the green (front, left, and back) and comes as close to an island green as you can get. The 447-yard par 5 sixth is the longest on the course and features a narrow fairway with thick woods along the left side. The nontraditional-looking clubhouse is mostly a pro shop and large restaurant. A miniature golf facility is available for those people who have yet to take up the game—or perhaps for those frustrated by it.

COURSES NEARBY: Bangor Municipal, Hampden, Hermon Meadows, Lucerne-in-Maine, Penobscot Valley, Pine Hill

FORT KENT GOLF CLUB
ST. JOHN ROAD
FORT KENT
207-834-3149

REGION: Aroostook

MAP: 67

ESTABLISHED: 1969

NUMBER OF HOLES: 9

COURSE LENGTH/PAR: Back: 6,367/71 **Front:** 5,361/72

COURSE RATING/SLOPE: Back: 69.0/111 **Front:** NA

HEAD PROFESSIONAL: Yes

COURSE ARCHITECT: Ben Gray

GOLF FACILITIES: Full pro shop, driving range, practice green, practice bunker, club rental, club repair, club storage, cart rental, pull-cart rental, instruction, locker room, showers, restaurant, lounge

TEE TIMES: Not necessary

RANGER: Yes

TIME TO PLAY 18 HOLES: 4 hours

EARLIEST TEE-OFF: 6 a.m.

GREEN FEES: Weekend (18): $ Weekday (18): $

PAYMENT: MasterCard, Visa

SEASON: Mid-April through October

LOCAL CHAMBER OF COMMERCE: Greater Fort Kent Area, 207-834-5354

LOCAL ATTRACTIONS: St. John River, Canadian border crossing

DIRECTIONS: The course is 3 miles outside Fort Kent on Route 161, on your left.

COURSE DESCRIPTION: Maine's northernmost golf course, Fort Kent Golf Club sits high on a former potato farm overlooking the St. John River and Canada. Touted locally as "the best-groomed course in Aroostook County," it's a fairly wide-open layout with rolling fairways and small greens. They are tough targets—well guarded by bumps and bunkers—and will test most players' short games. The 406-yard first earns its number one handicap rating by virtue of the fact that it runs uphill to a fairly flat green, with small bunkers ready for an errant approach. But it's the finishing holes—the 437-yard par-4 eighth and the 542-

yard par-5 ninth—that will add drama to your round. The eighth starts off from an elevated tee to a generous landing area. What's left is a long, blind approach to a small green. By contrast, the final hole is a slight dogleg right off the tee. Drive over the trees on the right and you're faced with a downhill second shot toward a large green with water to the right. For big hitters the green is reachable in two, affording the opportunity to reclaim what you may have lost at eight. Renovations are planned to expand the lounge area in the clubhouse.

COURSES NEARBY: Birch Point

FOXCROFT GOLF CLUB
36 FOXCROFT CENTER ROAD
DOVER-FOXCROFT
207-564-8887
REGION: Katahdin/Moosehead Region
MAP: 32
ESTABLISHED: 1965
NUMBER OF HOLES: 9
COURSE LENGTH/PAR: Back: 6,123/72   **Front:** 5,526/74
COURSE RATING/SLOPE: Back: 66.1/107 **Front:** 67.0/101
HEAD PROFESSIONAL: Yes
COURSE ARCHITECT: NA
GOLF FACILITIES: Full pro shop, practice green, club rental, cart rental, pull-cart rental, instruction, snack bar
TEE TIMES: Not necessary
RANGER: No
TIME TO PLAY 18 HOLES: 3 hours, 30 minutes
EARLIEST TEE-OFF: Daylight
GREEN FEES: Weekend (18): $ Weekday (18): $
PAYMENT: Cash only
SEASON: May 1 through October 1
LOCAL CHAMBER OF COMMERCE: Southern Piscataquis County, 207-564-7533
LOCAL ATTRACTIONS: Sebec Lake
DIRECTIONS: From Exit 39 off I-95 in Newport, follow Route 7 North to Dover-Foxcroft (or take Route 15 from Bangor). Turn right onto Route 16. The course is approximately 1½ miles from the post office.
COURSE DESCRIPTION: Tree-lined fairways and changes in terrain create the necessary challenge at this 6,123-yard layout. Three long par-4s—the 439-yard second, 428-yard third, and 401-yard eighth—require long approaches into small greens. Driving accuracy and good iron play are rewarded here. This is a well-maintained course, a testament to its dedicated owners. Its quiet, friendly atmosphere reflects the tradition and warmth of old Maine.
COURSES NEARBY: Dexter Municipal, Katahdin, Piscataquis, Todd Valley, Whitetail

FREEPORT COUNTRY CLUB
2 OLD COUNTY ROAD
FREEPORT
207-865-4922

REGION: Greater Portland Area
MAP: 6
ESTABLISHED: 1968
NUMBER OF HOLES: 9
COURSE LENGTH/PAR: Back: 5,894/72   **Front:** 4,808/72
COURSE RATING/SLOPE: Back: 69.0/116 **Front:** 67.1/109
HEAD PROFESSIONAL: No
COURSE ARCHITECT: NA
GOLF FACILITIES: Full pro shop, practice green, club rental, club repair, cart rental, pull-cart rental, snack bar
TEE TIMES: Recommended
RANGER: No
TEE-OFF INTERVAL TIME: 8 minutes
TIME TO PLAY 18 HOLES: 4 hours
EARLIEST TEE-OFF: 7 a.m.
GREEN FEES: Weekend (18): $ Weekday (18): $
PAYMENT: MasterCard, Visa
SEASON: Mid-April through November 15
LOCAL CHAMBER OF COMMERCE: Greater Portland Region, 207-772-2811
LOCAL ATTRACTIONS: L. L. Bean, Freeport shopping
DIRECTIONS: Take Exit 17 off I-95. Go past the Visitor Information Center. Take a left onto Old County Road, cross I-95, and take the first right to the course.
COURSE DESCRIPTION: Close to L. L. Bean, the course is visible from Route 95 just south of Freeport. It's fairly open, and its flat starting holes are balanced by the fourth through eighth, which wind their way through woods and water. A rolling fairway and sharp dogleg don't make the relatively short 418-yard fifth an easy par-5. The sixth is a manageable 177-yard par-3, unless of course your tee shot catches the gully on either side of the green. The approach at the 306-yard par-4 seventh is slightly uphill and over water. The same water comes into play on the eighth, a 156-yard par-3. Due in part to its proximity to a major shopping mecca, Freeport Golf Course is popular retreat for out-of-town visitors.
COURSES NEARBY: Brunswick, Mere Creek, Val Halla

FRYE ISLAND GOLF CLUB
FRYE ISLAND
207-655-4551
WEB SITE: www.fryeisland.com

REGION: Western Lakes and Mountains
MAP: 5
ESTABLISHED: 1972
NUMBER OF HOLES: 9
COURSE LENGTH/PAR: Back: 6,278/72   **Front:** 5,302/72
COURSE RATING/SLOPE: Back: 70.0/123 **Front:** 72.4/126
HEAD PROFESSIONAL: No
COURSE ARCHITECT: Geoffrey Cornish
GOLF FACILITIES: Practice net, club rental, club storage, cart rental, pull-cart rental, snack bar, lounge
TEE TIMES: Recommended
HOW LONG IN ADVANCE: 1 day
RANGER: Yes
TEE-OFF INTERVAL TIME: 10 minutes
TIME TO PLAY 18 HOLES: 4 hours, 30 minutes
EARLIEST TEE-OFF: 7:30 a.m.
GREEN FEES: Weekend (18): $$ **Weekday (18): $**
PAYMENT: Cash only
SEASON: May 1 through October 31
LOCAL CHAMBER OF COMMERCE: Greater Windham, 207-892-8265
LOCAL ATTRACTIONS: Sebago Lake, swimming, boating, camping
DIRECTIONS: From Portland take Route 302 through Raymond. About 2 miles past the intersection with Route 121, take a left onto Raymond Cape Road and follow this to the ferry landing. Once you're on the island, follow signs to the course.

COURSE DESCRIPTION: This Geoffrey Cornish–designed course located on an island in Sebago Lake is accessible only by ferry. Though it takes a little more effort to get here, those who endeavor will be well rewarded. Narrow tree-lined fairways and sloping greens are the norm, and there are plenty of opportunities for trouble. The 481-yard par-5 second is a good example. A pond begins about 215 yards out and extends nearly 90 yards down the left side of the fairway. The large green is actually a double green shared with the sixth. Interestingly, while number two is considered the hardest on the course, the 293-yard par-4 sixth is one of the easiest—if you're not intimidated by the ponds running along the left side and one that borders the right front of the green. The club's signature hole, the picturesque 170-yard par-3 eighth, requires a tee shot over water to a green guarded by three bunkers. Frye Island has limited accommodations, so be sure to call ahead and be aware of the ferry schedule.

COURSES NEARBY: Bridgton Highlands, Naples, Point Sebago, Spring Meadows,

Golf at Province Lake

Route 153

Parsonfield

800-325-4434

Region: Western Lakes and Mountains

Map: 4

Established: 1919

Number of Holes: 18

Course Length/Par: Back: 6,082/71 **Middle:** 5,742/71 **Front:** 4,874/71

Course Rating/Slope: Back: 70.1/127 **Middle:** 68.4/124 **Front:** 70.8/120

Head Professional: Yes

Course Architect: Lawrence Van Etten (O9), Brian Silva (A9)

Golf Facilities: Full pro shop, driving range, practice green, practice bunker, club rental, club repair, club storage, cart rental, pull-cart rental, instruction, locker room, showers, restaurant, lounge

Tee Times: Recommended

How Long in Advance: 5 days

Ranger: Yes

Tee-Off Interval Time: 8 minutes

Time to Play 18 Holes: 4 hours, 15 minutes

Earliest Tee-Off: Sunrise

Green Fees: Weekend (18): $$$ **Weekday (18): $$**

Payment: MasterCard, Visa

Season: Mid-April through early November

Local Chamber of Commerce: Bridgton Lakes Region, 207-647-3472

Local Attractions: Lakes, White Mountain National Forest

Directions: From Portland take Route 25 West to the New Hampshire border and an intersection with Route 153. Turn left onto Route 153. The course is 8½ miles ahead on your left.

Course Description: Located on the border of New Hampshire, a few holes straddle both states. In fact, on the 388-yard par-4 fourth, you'll tee off in Maine and putt in New Hampshire. The original nine opened in 1919. The back nine, designed by Brian Silva, was added in 1988. Under new management since 1996, all tees have been remodeled and some new tee boxes added, making holes more challenging for the good golfer and friendlier for the short hitter. The course starts out with six relatively open holes near the lake that give you a chance to warm up. The first hole has been recently extended, increasing it from a short 263-yard par-4 to a more formidable 395-yard opener (410 yards from the back tees). Starting with the seventh hole (requiring a tee shot over water), the course starts to wind through the trees and hills all the way through the eighteenth hole. Holes have all been given names reflective of their characteristics. The 129-yard par-3 fifth hole, for example, is called Bounce. No need to elaborate—just aim your drive left of the green. The back has lumps and bumps and well-contoured greens typical of a Silva design. The clubhouse and pro shop (a former farmhouse and barn) have been beautifully renovated. A tree-shaded outdoor patio provides a pleasant place to relax following your round. Carts are mandatory on weekends and holidays until 1 p.m.

COURSES NEARBY: West Newfield

GOOSE RIVER GOLF CLUB
50 PARK STREET
ROCKPORT
207-236-8488
REGION: Mid-Coast Region
MAP: 14
ESTABLISHED: 1965
NUMBER OF HOLES: 9
COURSE LENGTH/PAR: Back: 6,056/71   **Front:** 5,208/72
COURSE RATING/SLOPE: Back: 68.5/119 **Front:** NA
HEAD PROFESSIONAL: Yes
COURSE ARCHITECT: Cripps family
GOLF FACILITIES: Full pro shop, practice green, club rental, club repair, club storage, cart rental, pull-cart rental, instruction, snack bar, lounge
TEE TIMES: Recommended
HOW LONG IN ADVANCE: 1 week
RANGER: Yes
TEE-OFF INTERVAL TIME: 7 and 8 minutes
TIME TO PLAY 18 HOLES: 4 hours
EARLIEST TEE-OFF: 7 a.m.
GREEN FEES: Weekend (18): $$ **Weekday (18): $$**
PAYMENT: MasterCard, Visa
SEASON: Mid-April through October
LOCAL CHAMBER OF COMMERCE: Camden-Rockport-Lincolnville, 207-236-4404
LOCAL ATTRACTIONS: Camden, Mount Battie, windjammers, kayaking, hiking, shopping
DIRECTIONS: From Route 1 in Rockport take Route 90 West. After about 2 miles turn right onto Meadow Street (which becomes Simonton Road). Travel 2 miles. The course is on your right.
COURSE DESCRIPTION: A nine-hole course located near the popular tourist destination of Camden. Hilly terrain creates some elevated tees, uphill fairways and blind approaches. There are few bunkers, but the meandering Goose River comes into play on several holes. The number one handicap hole, the 581-yard first, gets you right into the swing of things. A mis-hit drive requires a well-hit second to carry the water that bisects the fairway. Different tees for the inward nine give a new look to some holes. The 495-yard par-5 fifth hole, for example, shortens to a

422-yard par-4 as the fourteenth. Both play steeply uphill to an elevated green, making either hole play much longer than its yardage. However, the view of the nearby Camden Hills from the green is worth the climb. A small clubhouse is nicely situated overlooking the course.

COURSES NEARBY: Samoset, Rockland, Northport

GORHAM COUNTRY CLUB

134 McLELLAN ROAD
GORHAM
207-839-3490
REGION: Greater Portland Area
MAP: 3
ESTABLISHED: 1961
NUMBER OF HOLES: 18
COURSE LENGTH/PAR: Back: 6,552/71   **Middle:** 6,334/71   **Front:** 5,426/72
COURSE RATING/SLOPE: Back: 70.1/120 **Middle:** 68.3/116   **Front:** 70.5/117
HEAD PROFESSIONAL: Yes
COURSE ARCHITECT: James MacDonald Sr.
GOLF FACILITIES: Full pro shop, driving range, practice green, club rental, club repair, club storage, cart rental, pull-cart rental, instruction, locker room, showers, restaurant, lounge
TEE TIMES: Recommended
HOW LONG IN ADVANCE: 3 days
RANGER: Yes
TEE-OFF INTERVAL TIME: 8 minutes
TIME TO PLAY 18 HOLES: 4 hours
EARLIEST TEE-OFF: 6:30 a.m.
GREEN FEES: Weekend (18): $$ Weekday (18): $$
PAYMENT: Cash only
SEASON: April 15 through November 15
LOCAL CHAMBER OF COMMERCE: Greater Portland Region, 207-772-2811
LOCAL ATTRACTIONS: Maine Mall, Portland
DIRECTIONS: From Exit 6 off the Maine Turnpike (I-95) turn left onto Payne Road. After about 1 mile take a left onto Route 114 (Gorham Road). Route 114 joins briefly with Route 22; turn right to stay on Route 114. McLellan Road is about 1/2 mile ahead on your right.
COURSE DESCRIPTION: Just west of Portland, Gorham Country Club is a locally designed course that has developed a fine reputation among southern Maine golfers. In past years it has played host to the Maine Open. Headlining this fairly tight, tree-lined layout is the 369-yard par-4 third hole. This dogleg left requires a downhill approach that needs to clear a creek that runs in front of the small green. Water also comes into play on the 500-yard par-5 eighteenth, regarded by

many as one of the nicest finishing holes around. It's an uphill dogleg left; a pond will catch a mis-hit second shot. The 424-yard fourteenth is considered the best on the course. Standing on the tee looking down the narrow, right-to-left-sloping fairway that doglegs to the left, it is easy to be intimidated. But take solace in the fact that you're not alone.

COURSES NEARBY: Nonesuch River, Pleasant Hill, Rivermeadow, Riverside Municipal, Sable Oaks, Salmon Falls, South Portland Municipal, Twin Falls, Val Halla, Westerly Winds, Willowdale

GREAT COVE GOLF CLUB
ROQUE BLUFFS ROAD
ROQUE BLUFFS
207-434-2981
REGION: Acadia/Down East
MAP: 26
ESTABLISHED: 1977
NUMBER OF HOLES: 9
COURSE LENGTH/PAR: Back: 3,388/60   **Front:** 2,680/66
COURSE RATING/SLOPE: Back: 55.1/84   **Front:** NA
HEAD PROFESSIONAL: No
COURSE ARCHITECT: Paul Browne
GOLF FACILITIES: Driving range, practice green, club rental, cart rental, pull-cart rental, snack bar
TEE TIMES: Not necessary
RANGER: No
TIME TO PLAY 18 HOLES: 3 hours
EARLIEST TEE-OFF: 7 a.m.
GREEN FEES: Weekend (18): $ Weekday (18): $
PAYMENT: Cash only
SEASON: May through September
LOCAL CHAMBER OF COMMERCE: Machias Bay Area, 207-255-4402
LOCAL ATTRACTIONS: Roque Bluffs State Park
DIRECTIONS: The course is 3 miles off Route 1 from Jonesboro on Roque Bluffs Road.
COURSE DESCRIPTION: This is down east Maine at its best. About as far from the madding crowd as you can get, sits this short oceanside track overlooking Great Cove and Englishman Bay. Legend has it that this area and nearby Machias were a summer retreat for 18th-century pirates. Just on the other side of the bay is Jonesport, birthplace of the classic Maine lobster-boat style of the same name. Short par-4s (the longest is the 306-yard first) are nicely balanced by a couple of long par-3s at the 176-yard second and the 182-yard eighth. But difficulty is not the leading attraction here. This is one of Maine's hidden gems where golf is

played for golf's sake in an idyllic, uncrowded setting. The green fee lets you play all day. And you may very well want to.

COURSES NEARBY: St. Croix

GREEN VALLEY GOLF CLUB

ROUTE 2

ENFIELD

207-732-3006

E-MAIL: gvgc@telplus.net

REGION: Katahdin/Moosehead Region

MAP: 33

ESTABLISHED: 1965

NUMBER OF HOLES: 9

COURSE LENGTH/PAR: Back: 5,648/70   **Front:** 4,840/70

COURSE RATING/SLOPE: Back: 65.8/112 **Front:** NA

HEAD PROFESSIONAL: No

COURSE ARCHITECT: NA

GOLF FACILITIES: Driving range, practice green, club rental, cart rental, pull-cart rental, snack bar

TEE TIMES: Not necessary

RANGER: No

TIME TO PLAY 18 HOLES: 4 hours

EARLIEST TEE-OFF: 7 a.m.

GREEN FEES: Weekend (18): $ Weekday (18): $

PAYMENT: MasterCard, Visa

SEASON: Late April through late October

LOCAL CHAMBER OF COMMERCE: Greater Lincoln Area, 207-794-8065

LOCAL ATTRACTIONS: Lakes, fishing

DIRECTIONS: From Bangor take I-95 North to Exit 54. Turn right onto Route 155 to West Enfield, then left onto Route 2 North. The course is 4½ miles ahead.

COURSE DESCRIPTION: Green Valley is a wide-open track, fairly flat but with small, challenging greens. Despite its proximity to Bangor—it's just 40 minutes north—most play comes from local communities. It is a laid-back crowd who appreciates the layout's forgiving nature. The 363-yard par-4 fifth will require the most skill. It's a dogleg left; a brook runs across the fairway at the corner about 200 yards out. It's uphill from there to a tiered green with bunkers left and right. As with most holes on the course, placing your approach on the small green may not be as easy as it first appears.

COURSES NEARBY: Hidden Meadows, Jato Highlands

GRINDSTONE NECK GOLF COURSE

GRINDSTONE AVENUE
WINTER HARBOR
207-963-7760
REGION: Acadia/Down East
MAP: 17
ESTABLISHED: 1891
NUMBER OF HOLES: 9
COURSE LENGTH/PAR: Back: 6,190/72   **Front:** 5,100/72
COURSE RATING/SLOPE: Back: NA   **Front:** NA
HEAD PROFESSIONAL: No
COURSE ARCHITECT: Alex Findlay, Charlie Clark
GOLF FACILITIES: Full pro shop, club rental, club storage, pull-cart rental
TEE TIMES: Not necessary
RANGER: No
TEE-OFF INTERVAL TIME: 8 minutes
TIME TO PLAY 18 HOLES: 4 hours
EARLIEST TEE-OFF: Sunrise
GREEN FEES: Weekend (18): $$$ **Weekday (18): $$**
PAYMENT: Cash only
SEASON: June 1 through mid-October
LOCAL CHAMBER OF COMMERCE: Ellsworth Area, 207-667-5584
LOCAL ATTRACTIONS: Schoodic Peninsula, Acadia National Park
DIRECTIONS: From Ellsworth take Route 1 North. Turn right onto Route 186 to Winter Harbor. Take a right at the stop sign. About 1/2 mile ahead take a left onto Grindstone Avenue. The club is 1/2 mile ahead on your right.
COURSE DESCRIPTION: Established in 1891, Grindstone Neck is one of the oldest golf clubs in Maine. The original nine holes (built in 1895) were laid by Alex Findlay. The current track, which has since expanded to both sides of Grindstone Avenue, was designed by Charles Clark in 1925. Members proudly claim Grindstone Neck as the only nine-hole course in the United States where the ocean is visible on every hole. In fact, the greens on the 340-yard second and the 317-yard third (a sharp dogleg left) are virtually on the beach. Views of Frenchman Bay with Ironbound, Jordan, and Mount Desert Islands in the distance are spectacular. This is a vintage layout. The rough is truly rough (no 2-inch grass here), and the greens are small and contoured. Elevation sometimes makes them tough targets, as is the case with the 335-yard sixth. The back-to-front-sloping green with trees in back leaves little room for error. The small clubhouse is new and has a comfortable porch to relax. But food and beverage service is only available in town.
COURSES NEARBY: Bar Harbor, Blink Bonnie, White Birches

HAMPDEN COUNTRY CLUB

25 THOMAS ROAD
HAMPDEN
207-862-9999
REGION: Katahdin/Moosehead Region
MAP: 23
ESTABLISHED: 1967
NUMBER OF HOLES: 9
COURSE LENGTH/PAR: Back: 5,518/72   **Front:** 5,100/72
COURSE RATING/SLOPE: Back: NA/108   **Front:** NA/112
HEAD PROFESSIONAL: No
COURSE ARCHITECT: Hamm Robbins
GOLF FACILITIES: Practice green, practice bunker, club rental, club repair, club storage, cart rental, pull-cart rental, locker room, snack bar
TEE TIMES: Not necessary
RANGER: No
TIME TO PLAY 18 HOLES: 4 hours
EARLIEST TEE-OFF: 7 a.m.
GREEN FEES: Weekend (18): $ Weekday (18): $
PAYMENT: Cash only
SEASON: Snowmelt to snowfall
LOCAL CHAMBER OF COMMERCE: Bangor Region, 207-947-0307
LOCAL ATTRACTIONS: Greater Bangor area
DIRECTIONS: From Exit 43 off I-95 head south on Route 69 to Route 9. Take a left onto Route 9. Thomas Road is 3 miles ahead on your right; the course is at the end of the road.
COURSE DESCRIPTION: One of the least-pretentious "country clubs" in the state. A short, open layout, it was built in 1967 and has been owned and operated by the Gamble family since 1970. Generous landing areas are tempered by small greens. Although relatively short, the par-5s—the seventh and ninth holes (462 and 420 yards, respectively)—are not forgone birdie opportunities. A large pine tree blocks your approach to a small sloping green on seven that is further guarded by a mound and bunker. The ninth, too, has a small undulating target that is tucked close to woods along the right and back and has a bunker left of the green. Another nine holes (designed by Dean Gamble) has already been cleared; plans are to have it in play by 2000. The original nine will be incorporated into it. The new layout promises to be much tighter with more doglegs.
COURSES NEARBY: Bangor Municipal, Felt Brook, Kenduskeag, Hermon Meadows, Penobscot Valley, Pine Hill, Streamside

HERMON MEADOWS GOLF CLUB
BILLINGS ROAD
HERMON
207-848-3741
REGION: Katahdin/Moosehead Region
MAP: 23
ESTABLISHED: 1964
NUMBER OF HOLES: 18
COURSE LENGTH/PAR: Back: 6,329/72   **Middle:** 5,895/72   **Front:** 5,395/72
COURSE RATING/SLOPE: Back: 69.4/117   **Middle:** 67.7/113   **Front:** 70.9/120
HEAD PROFESSIONAL: Yes
COURSE ARCHITECT: Wynn Pike
GOLF FACILITIES: Full pro shop, driving range, practice green, club rental, club repair, club storage, cart rental, pull-cart rental, instruction, locker room, restaurant, lounge
TEE TIMES: Recommended
HOW LONG IN ADVANCE: 1 day
RANGER: Yes
TEE-OFF INTERVAL TIME: 8 minutes
TIME TO PLAY 18 HOLES: 4 hours
EARLIEST TEE-OFF: Dawn
GREEN FEES: Weekend (18): $$ **Weekday (18): $$**
PAYMENT: MasterCard, Visa, American Express
SEASON: April till snow
LOCAL CHAMBER OF COMMERCE: Bangor Region, 207-947-0307
LOCAL ATTRACTIONS: Greater Bangor area
DIRECTIONS: From Bangor take Route 222 west to Hermon. Turn right onto Billings Road.

COURSE DESCRIPTION: This is a fairly open course west of Bangor with rolling terrain, a couple of sharp doglegs, and plenty of water. Greens are small and well maintained. Several have two or more bunkers guarding them, so accuracy is the name of the game here. The par-5 sixth is the number one handicap hole on the front, not only because of its 545-yard length but because of a large pond that sits about 120 yards from the smallest green on the course. It will make even the biggest hitters think twice about going for it in two. Number eight is just 165 yards, but it's uphill to a small green that is closely guarded on the right and left by trees, making for a tough target. Locals have appropriately dubbed the fourteenth "Big Tree in the Way" because of the large pine tree that stands on the corner of this 320-yard dogleg right. Even a good drive may leave an approach that is partially blocked. The 510-yard par-5 15th is an interesting double dogleg. The club recently opened a new grass practice tee—one of the largest in the state. Newly paved cart paths will allow them to offer cart play earlier in the season.

COURSES NEARBY: Bangor Municipal, Carmel Valley, Felt Brook, Hampden, Kenduskeag, Penobscot Valley, Pine Hill

HIDDEN MEADOWS GOLF COURSE
ROUTE 43
OLD TOWN
207-827-2751
REGION: Katahdin/Moosehead Region
MAP: 33
ESTABLISHED: 1997
NUMBER OF HOLES: 9
COURSE LENGTH/PAR: Back: 5,640/72   **Front:** 5,146/72
COURSE RATING/SLOPE: Back: 66.1/102 **Front:** NA
HEAD PROFESSIONAL: No
COURSE ARCHITECT: Jeff and James Dufour
GOLF FACILITIES: Club rental, cart rental, pull-cart rental
TEE TIMES: Not necessary
RANGER: No
TIME TO PLAY 18 HOLES: 3 hours
EARLIEST TEE-OFF: 7 a.m.
GREEN FEES: Weekend (18): $ Weekday (18): $
PAYMENT: Cash only
SEASON: May 15 through October 12
LOCAL CHAMBER OF COMMERCE: Bangor Region, 207-947-0307
LOCAL ATTRACTIONS: University of Maine, Penobscot Indian Reservation, Greater Bangor area
DIRECTIONS: Take Exit 52 off I-95 and turn left off the ramp. The course is about 1/2 mile ahead.
COURSE DESCRIPTION: Designed and built by the Dufour family, this nine-hole layout occupies land that was once hay fields. In fact, areas between the first and second holes still are. The owners like to say there is fairway, then rough, and then "rough-rough." A short course, it has its fair share of challenges—primarily in the form of an alder swamp that runs along the right side of the 393-yard par-5 seventh hole. It is a sharp dogleg, so trying to cut the corner is not recommended. Wetlands also need to be cleared on the tee shot at the 370-yard fifth. The owners admit Hidden Meadows is a work in progress.
COURSES NEARBY: Bangor Municipal, Green Valley, Kenduskeag Valley, Penobscot Valley, Todd Valley

HIGHLAND LINKS GOLF CLUB
301 CIDER HILL ROAD
YORK
207-351-2727
WEB: www.highlandlinks.com

Region: Southern Coast
Map: 1
Established: 1995
Number of Holes: 9
Course Length/Par: Back: 5,594/70   **Front:** 4,758/70
Course Rating/Slope: Back: 65.4/110 **Front:** NA
Head Professional: No
Course Architect: NA
Golf Facilities: Full pro shop, driving range, practice green, practice bunker, club rental, club repair, cart rental, pull-cart rental, instruction, snack bar
Tee Times: Recommended
How Long in Advance: 2 days
Ranger: No
Tee-Off Interval Time: 15 minutes
Time to Play 18 Holes: 4 hours
Earliest Tee-Off: 7 a.m.
Green Fees: Weekend (18): $$ **Weekday (18):** $$
Payment: Cash only
Season: Mid-April through mid-November
Local Chamber of Commerce: The Yorks, 207-363-4422
Local Attractions: Southern Maine beaches, historic sites, Kittery outlet stores
Directions: Heading north on I-95, take Exit 4 (use Exit 1 if traveling south). Turn right onto Route 1 South, then right onto Route 91 North. The course is about 3 miles ahead on your right.
Course Description: A wide-open links-style layout that is easy to walk and popular with seniors and juniors. It's not a long course, but accuracy is necessary on approaches to the small, heavily bunkered greens. Water comes into play on two holes, most notably the 110-yard sixth. A horseshoe-shaped pond protects the front of the small target green. At 265 yards, the tree-lined par-4 ninth requires accuracy off the tee as well as concern for the strategically placed pond, which may make a short hitter think about laying up. This is a pretty setting in a historic area.
Courses Nearby: Cape Neddick, The Ledges, Links at Outlook, Sanford

Hillcrest Golf Club
82 Westwood Avenue
Millinocket
207-723-8410
Region: Katahdin/Moosehead Region
Map: 43
Established: 1930

NUMBER OF HOLES: 9

COURSE LENGTH/PAR: Back: 4,954/66 **Front:** 4,380/72

COURSE RATING/SLOPE: Back: 63.2/104 **Front:** 63.9/97

HEAD PROFESSIONAL: Yes

COURSE ARCHITECT: NA

GOLF FACILITIES: Full pro shop, practice green, club rental, cart rental, pull-cart rental, instruction, snack bar

TEE TIMES: Not necessary

RANGER: No

TIME TO PLAY 18 HOLES: 4 hours

EARLIEST TEE-OFF: 7 a.m.

GREEN FEES: Weekend (18): $ Weekday (18): $

PAYMENT: MasterCard, Visa

SEASON: May 1 through mid-October

LOCAL CHAMBER OF COMMERCE: Katahdin Area, 207-723-4443

LOCAL ATTRACTIONS: Baxter State Park, Mount Katahdin, hiking, lakes

DIRECTIONS: From Exit 56 (Medway) off I-95. Turn left onto Route 157 and drive approximately 15 miles to Millinocket. The course is located behind Stearns High School.

COURSE DESCRIPTION: This short, picturesque, nine-hole layout is just 35 minutes from Baxter State Park. It sits virtually in the shadow of Maine's highest peak, 5,267-foot Mount Katahdin, which is clearly visible from the sixth tee. This 401-yard par-4—longest on the course—is typical, with a rolling fairway that yields few level lies. The tee shot on the 221-yard par-3 seventh normally plays into a headwind, so even a long hitter will need a long iron or even a driver. There's no water on the course but lots of rock ledge in the rough. As the only golf course for 30 miles, Hillcrest can be quite busy, especially on weekends.

COURSES NEARBY: Va Jo Wa

HOULTON COMMUNITY GOLF COURSE

NICKERSON LAKE ROAD

HOULTON

207-532-2662

REGION: Aroostook

MAP: 53

ESTABLISHED: 1917

NUMBER OF HOLES: 9

COURSE LENGTH/PAR: Back: 5,727/72 **Front:** 5,344/76

COURSE RATING/SLOPE: Back: 68.7/117 **Front:** 70.6/117

HEAD PROFESSIONAL: No

COURSE ARCHITECT: NA

GOLF FACILITIES: Full pro shop, driving range, practice bunker, club rental, club repair, cart rental, pull-cart rental, instruction, locker room, showers, snack bar, lounge

TEE TIMES: Not necessary

RANGER: No

TIME TO PLAY 18 HOLES: 4 hours

EARLIEST TEE-OFF: 7 a.m.

GREEN FEES: Weekend (18): $$ **Weekday (18): $**

PAYMENT: Cash only

SEASON: Mid-May through mid-October

LOCAL CHAMBER OF COMMERCE: Greater Houlton, 207-532-4216

LOCAL ATTRACTIONS: Watson Settlement covered bridge, Canadian border crossing

DIRECTIONS: From Exit 65 off I-95 follow Route 2 toward Houlton for about 5 miles. Take a right onto Station Road and follow to its end. Take a left onto Nickerson Lake Road. The course is on your right.

COURSE DESCRIPTION: Golf has been played in The County since 1917, when a group of Houlton-area doctors and lawyers got together and formed Houlton Community Golf Course. The designer of record has been lost to time, but except for a few new tee boxes and a new ninth green, this nine-hole track plays true to its original layout. Built on a former potato farm (as several of Aroostook's courses are), Houlton is an open course with generous landing areas. There are 9 holes but 10 greens. (The ninth and eighteenth play to two different greens.) The only trees you'll encounter are those planted by members over the years. Some of them help define the 350-yard ninth hole, which plays as a downhill dogleg left to a green tucked into a stand of spruce and pine. Most holes are straightaway, but hills, fairway contours, and small, elevated greens can present challenging lies and blind approaches. The clubhouse, built in 1926, sits overlooking Nickerson Lake and still maintains its 1920s charm.

COURSES NEARBY: Mars Hill, Va Jo Wa,

ISLAND COUNTRY CLUB
ROUTE 15A
SUNSET
207-348-2379

REGION: Acadia/Down East

MAP: 15

ESTABLISHED: 1927

NUMBER OF HOLES: 9

COURSE LENGTH/PAR: Back: 3,865/62   **Front:** 3,624/64

COURSE RATING/SLOPE: Back: 58.8/97   **Front:** 62.1/92

HEAD PROFESSIONAL: Yes

COURSE ARCHITECT: N.A.

GOLF FACILITIES: Practice green, club rental, club storage, cart rental, pull-cart

rental, instruction, snack bar

TEE TIMES: Not necessary

RANGER: No

TIME TO PLAY 18 HOLES: 3 hours

EARLIEST TEE-OFF: 6:30 a.m.

GREEN FEES: Weekend (18): $$ **Weekday (18): $**

PAYMENT: Cash only

SEASON: Memorial Day through September

LOCAL CHAMBER OF COMMERCE: Ellsworth Area, 207-667-5584

LOCAL ATTRACTIONS: Scenery, lobster-boat races, Stonington, Isle au Haut

DIRECTIONS: From Belfast take Route 1 North to Route 15 South (Orland). Follow Route 15 to Deer Isle village. Take a right, and the course is 2 miles ahead on your left.

COURSE DESCRIPTION: The drive down Route 15 to Island Country Club on Deer Isle is one of the prettiest in the state. The firm of Stiles & Van Kleek drew up plans for a course here, but for unknown reasons the design was never implemented. The current layout is said to be the collaboration of several early club members, and the result is a charming, albeit short track. Newcomers will want to remember that the 251-yard second hole is a dogleg right leading uphill toward the clubhouse. (The green that's visible straight ahead from the tee is the seventh.) A string of par-3s with distances ranging from 114 to 199 yards—the third through the seventh—will require all varieties of shot-making skills. Saving the best for last, the eighth and ninth play across the side of a hill. From the tee at eight (318 yards) the hole appears narrow, with trees right and leading down to the right-to-left-sloping fairway. But it opens up about 150 yards out, leaving a short approach to a tiered green with woods close to the right and back. At 323 yards, the ninth is slightly longer and uphill; the fairway slopes left to right on this dogleg right. A newly expanded clubhouse is very comfortable and the atmosphere friendly. The green fee allows you to play all day.

COURSES NEARBY: Castine

J. W. PARKS GOLF COURSE

94 HARTLAND AVENUE

PITTSFIELD

207-487-5545

REGION: Kennebec/Moose River Region

MAP: 21

ESTABLISHED: 1964

NUMBER OF HOLES: 9

COURSE LENGTH/PAR: Back: 5,803/70   **Front:** 5,114/70

COURSE RATING/SLOPE: Back: 68.3/119 **Front:** 68.1/111

HEAD PROFESSIONAL: Yes

COURSE ARCHITECT: John Dana

GOLF FACILITIES: Full pro shop, driving range, practice green, club rental, club repair, cart rental, pull-cart rental, instruction, snack bar, lounge

TEE TIMES: Not necessary

RANGER: No

TIME TO PLAY 18 HOLES: 4 hours

EARLIEST TEE-OFF: 7 a.m.

GREEN FEES: Weekend (18): $ Weekday (18): $

PAYMENT: MasterCard, Visa, American Express

SEASON: April 1 through November 1

LOCAL CHAMBER OF COMMERCE: Mid-Maine, 207-873-3315 or 3316

LOCAL ATTRACTIONS: Sebasticook Lake (Newport), Maine Central Institute

DIRECTIONS: From Waterville take exit 38 off I-95. Turn right off the ramp toward Pittsfield, then left onto Route 152. The course is about 1 mile ahead on your left.

COURSE DESCRIPTION: Equidistant between Waterville and Bangor, J. W. Parks is only minutes off I-95. Each hole on this nine-hole layout has two sets of tees, resulting in a "front" nine that measures slightly shorter than than the "back." In fact, two holes actually change par. The 375-yard par-4 first becomes a 436-yard par-5 when you turn the corner; conversely, the 492-yard par-5 3rd becomes a challenging 412-yard par-4 twelfth hole with bunkers guarding either side of the tiered green. Water is in play on holes five through seven, including the entire length of the 268-yard sixth. There is plenty of opportunity to score well here, but with ample woods and water and some well-placed bunkers, the course provides challenges for all levels. There is a good-size lounge and snack bar.

COURSES NEARBY: Lakeview, Orchard View, Palmyra,

JATO HIGHLANDS GOLF CLUB

TOWN FARM ROAD

LINCOLN

207-794-2433

REGION: Katahdin/Moosehead Region

MAP: 44

ESTABLISHED: 1999

NUMBER OF HOLES: 9 (expanding to 18 in 2000)

COURSE LENGTH/PAR: Back: 5,915/72   **Middle:** 5,608/72   **Front:** 4,786/72

COURSE RATING/SLOPE: Back: 66.3/107 **Front:** NA

HEAD PROFESSIONAL: No

COURSE ARCHITECT: Tom Gardner

GOLF FACILITIES: Driving range, practice green, cart rental, pull-cart rental, snack bar

TEE TIMES: Recommended

HOW LONG IN ADVANCE: One month

RANGER: No

TEE-OFF INTERVAL TIME: 10 minutes

TIME TO PLAY 18 HOLES: 3 hours, 45 minutes

EARLIEST TEE-OFF: 7 a.m.

GREEN FEES: Weekend (18): $ Weekday (18): $

PAYMENT: MasterCard, Visa

SEASON: Mid-April through October

LOCAL CHAMBER OF COMMERCE: Greater Lincoln Area, 207-794-8065

LOCAL ATTRACTIONS: Lakes, fishing

DIRECTIONS: Take I-95 to Exit 55 and drive 4 miles to Route 2. Turn left and follow Route 2 about 5 miles to Town Farm Road, on your right. The course is 1 mile ahead on your right.

COURSE DESCRIPTION: The first nine holes of this new course were opened in the summer of 1999. A full 18 will be opened in 2000. (The course rating and slope are for nine holes.) Only a few holes cover what was once farmland; the rest have been cut through woods and feature some pretty dramatic elevation changes. The 305-yard par-4 seventh is a slight dogleg left. The tee is about 40 feet above the fairway and requires a shot over water. When completed, the par-3 tenth will have a 180-foot drop to the green. Plans also call for a new clubhouse with additional facilities.

COURSES NEARBY: Green Valley

KATAHDIN COUNTRY CLUB
PARK STREET
MILO
207- 943-2686

REGION: Katahdin/Moosehead Region

MAP: 32

ESTABLISHED: 1930

NUMBER OF HOLES: 9

COURSE LENGTH/PAR: Back: 6,006/72

COURSE RATING/SLOPE: Back: 65.8/103

HEAD PROFESSIONAL: No

COURSE ARCHITECT: Larry Striley

GOLF FACILITIES: Full pro shop, practice green, club rental, cart rental, pull-cart rental, snack bar

TEE TIMES: Not necessary

RANGER: No

TIME TO PLAY 18 HOLES: 3 hours, 50 minutes

EARLIEST TEE-OFF: Daylight

GREEN FEES: Weekend (18): $ Weekday (18): $

PAYMENT: Cash only

SEASON: Mid-April through October

LOCAL CHAMBER OF COMMERCE: Southern Piscataquis County, 207-564-7533

LOCAL ATTRACTIONS: Sebec Lake, Baxter State Park

DIRECTIONS: From Bangor take Exit 53 off I-95. Take Route 16 North to Milo. In town turn right onto Park Street by the cemetery. The course is 2 miles ahead on your left.

COURSE DESCRIPTION: On the edge of northern Maine's vast timberlands, Katahdin is an open layout featuring rolling fairways and small, well-maintained greens. Family owned and operated since 1940, it's popular with the locals. According to superintendent Rick Gerrish, sandy soil leaves the course "dry as a biscuit come spring," allowing it to be one of the first in the area to open for the season. While there's no water to contend with, hazards present themselves in other forms. The 485-yard par-5 sixth, for example, has a huge waste bunker that stretches across the fairway and comes into play on your second shot. The 447-yard par-4 eighth is straightaway, but a rolling fairway and small elevated green add to the challenge.

COURSES NEARBY: Foxcroft, Todd Valley, Whitetail

KEBO VALLEY CLUB
EAGLE LAKE ROAD
BAR HARBOR
207-288-5000

REGION: Acadia/Down East

MAP: 16

ESTABLISHED: 1888

NUMBER OF HOLES: 18

COURSE LENGTH/PAR: Back: 6,131/70   **Middle:** 5,933/70   **Front:** 5,440/72

COURSE RATING/SLOPE: Back: 69.0/130 **Middle:** 69.0/130   **Front:** 72.0/121

HEAD PROFESSIONAL: Yes

COURSE ARCHITECT: H. C. Leeds

GOLF FACILITIES: Full pro shop, practice green, practice bunker, club rental, club repair, club storage, cart rental, pull-cart rental, instruction, locker room, showers, restaurant, lounge

TEE TIMES: Necessary

HOW LONG IN ADVANCE: 3 days

RANGER: Yes

TEE-OFF INTERVAL TIME: 8 minutes

TIME TO PLAY 18 HOLES: 4 hours, 30 minutes

EARLIEST TEE-OFF: 6:30 a.m.

GREEN FEES: Weekend (18): $$$$ Weekday (18): $$$$

PAYMENT: MasterCard, Visa, American Express

SEASON: May 1 through October 30

Local Chamber of Commerce: Bangor Region, 207-947-0307

Local Attractions: Bar Harbor, Acadia National Park

Directions: From Ellsworth take Route 3 East to Route 233 and turn right. The course is on your left.

Course Description: Just minutes west of Bar Harbor, Kebo Valley Club was established in 1888, making it the eighth oldest club in America. Its first full 9 was opened in 1896, and its present 18-hole layout, designed by Herbert C. Leeds (whose credits include Myopia Club in Massachusetts), was built in 1919. Kebo maintains the reputation as one of the finest classic courses in the country. It has been selected several times—most recently in 1998—as site of the Maine Amateur. Set virtually in the shadow of Cadillac Mountain in nearby Acadia National Park, Kebo is not a long course (barely 6,000 yards) but plays to a tough par-70. The secret is position. You'll score well—or poorly—depending on where you leave your drive. From the narrow, rolling fairway at the 413-yard eighth (a hole Walter Hagen described as one of the best par 4s he ever played) to the trademark waste bunker that covers the entire slope leading up to the seventeenth green (a hazard from which President Howard Taft needed 23 strokes to get out), Kebo Valley is a history lesson that no student of the game should miss.

Courses Nearby: Bar Harbor, Causeway, Northeast Harbor,

KENDUSKEAG VALLEY GOLF COURSE

Grant Road

Kenduskeag

207-884-7330

Map: 32

Established: 1958

Number of Holes: 9

Course Length/Par: Back: 5,130/68 **Front:** 4,850/70

Course Rating/Slope: Back: 63.8/108 **Front:** 67.4/NA

Head Professional: No

Course Architect: Robert Girvan, Sr.

Golf Facilities: Club rental, club repair, cart rental, pull-cart rental, snack bar

Tee Times: Not necessary

Ranger: No

Time to Play 18 Holes: 3 hours

Earliest Tee-Off: 7 a.m.

Green Fees: Weekend (18): $ Weekday (18): $

Payment: Cash only

Season: Late April through early November

Local Chamber of Commerce: Bangor Region, 207-947-0307

Local Attractions: White-water canoe race

Directions: From Bangor take Exit 38 off I-95, then take Route 15 North through Kenduskeag. Follow Route 15 1⅓ miles from town and turn left onto Grant Road. The course is ½ mile ahead on your right.

COURSE DESCRIPTION: A short, open layout about 12 miles north and west of Bangor. A few holes border the Kenduskeag Stream, a well-known white-water canoe venue in the spring. In fact, the dogleg-right 483-yard par-5 third bends around the water hazard for its entire length, making a true three-shotter for most. Another dogleg, and the number one handicap hole, is the 420-yard seventh. If its length isn't challenging enough, a pond and double-tiered green will likely give pause. Very informal, country setting. The "pro shop" is an extra room in the owner's house.

COURSES NEARBY: Bangor Municipal, Carmel Valley, Hampden, Hermon Meadows, Hidden Meadows, Todd Valley, Whitetail

KENNEBEC HEIGHTS COUNTRY CLUB
ONE FAIRWAY LANE
FARMINGDALE
207-582-2000
REGION: Kennebec/Moose River Region
MAP: 12
ESTABLISHED: 1959
NUMBER OF HOLES: 18
COURSE LENGTH/PAR: Back: 6,003/70 **Middle:** 5,525/70 **Front:** 4,820/70
COURSE RATING/SLOPE: Back: 69.0/129 **Middle:** 67.1/123 **Front:** 67.7/119
HEAD PROFESSIONAL: No
COURSE ARCHITECT: Cornish & Silva (A9—1988)
GOLF FACILITIES: Full pro shop, driving range, practice green, practice bunker, club rental, club repair, cart rental, pull-cart rental, instruction, locker room, showers, snack bar
TEE TIMES: Necessary
HOW LONG IN ADVANCE: 1 week
RANGER: Yes
TEE-OFF INTERVAL TIME: 8 minutes
TIME TO PLAY 18 HOLES: 4 hours, 15 minutes
EARLIEST TEE-OFF: 6:30 a.m.
GREEN FEES: Weekend (18): $$ **Weekday (18): $$**
PAYMENT: MasterCard, Visa
SEASON: Mid-April through mid-November
LOCAL CHAMBER OF COMMERCE: Kennebec Valley, 207-623-4559
LOCAL ATTRACTIONS: State capitol building, government offices, Kennebec River
DIRECTIONS: Take Exit 28 off I-95 or Exit 14 off the Maine Turnpike (I-495), then follow Route 9/126 into Gardiner. Turn left onto Route 201. The course is about 1 mile ahead on your left. Look for a sign.

COURSE DESCRIPTION: Just minutes from Maine's capital city, the Kennebec Heights' front nine is open and rolling, presenting a broad profile and several sloping greens. The Kennebec River provides a nice backdrop to few holes, including the 185-yard par-3 sixth—which, with a large bunker to the right of an undulating green, doesn't give up many pars. The back nine (designed by Cornish & Silva), in contrast, was carved through woods; it's thereby tighter and features more sand and contoured greens. The 300-yard par-4 eleventh has water lining the left side of the fairway and a green tucked among bunkers and trees. The picturesque par 3 fifteenth is bisected by a small stream bordered by highbush blueberries lying in wait for mis-hit or short tee shots. The hole most talked about is the 392-yard par 4 seventeenth, known locally as Jake's Nightmare, after one of the club's founders. A narrow tree-lined fairway opens up to a good-size landing area, only to close in again around a narrow but deep green guarded by bunkers and other potential "nightmarish" problems.

COURSES NEARBY: Belgrade Lakes, Capitol City, Cobbossee Colony, The Meadows, Natanis, Western View

LAKE KEZAR COUNTRY CLUB

ROUTE 5
LOVELL
207-925-2462
REGION: Western Lakes and Mountains
MAP: 10
ESTABLISHED: 1923
NUMBER OF HOLES: 18
COURSE LENGTH/PAR: Back: 5,961/72   **Middle:** 5,585/72   **Front:** 5,088/72
COURSE RATING/SLOPE: Back: 67.3/117 **Middle:** 65.7/111   **Front:** 68.8/114
HEAD PROFESSIONAL: No
COURSE ARCHITECT: Donald Ross (O9), Brian Merrill (A9)
GOLF FACILITIES: Full pro shop, practice green, practice bunker, club rental, club repair, club storage, cart rental, pull-cart rental, snack bar
TEE TIMES: Recommended
HOW LONG IN ADVANCE: 5 days
RANGER: Yes
TEE-OFF INTERVAL TIME: 8 minutes
TIME TO PLAY 18 HOLES: 3 hours, 30 minutes
EARLIEST TEE-OFF: 7 a.m.
GREEN FEES: Weekend (18): $$ **Weekday (18): $$**
PAYMENT: Cash only
SEASON: May 1 through October
LOCAL CHAMBER OF COMMERCE: Bridgton Lakes Region, 207-647-3472
LOCAL ATTRACTIONS: Kezar Lake, fishing, hiking

DIRECTIONS: From Portland take Exit 8 off the Maine Turnpike (I-95). Follow Route 25 West to Standish. In about 2 miles bear right onto Route 113, which becomes Route 5 in Cornish. Follow Route 5 to Lovell. The course is 2 miles north of Lovell on your left.

COURSE DESCRIPTION: Founded by members of the area's wealthy summer community, Lake Kezar's front nine was designed by Donald Ross in 1923. Despite some modifications over the years, the course retains the charm of its vintage. It is a reasonably short layout; all greens are open in front and generally flat with subtle undulations. There are just a few bunkers. However, trouble—in the form of woods, out of bounds, or water—lurks down the right side of every hole on the front nine. Greens are tucked among towering white pines, so accuracy is important. The 275-yard par-4 fourth hole, for example, may be reachable for some, but the narrow, tree-lined fairway requires a straight drive. If you land in the trees, you'll have to hit sideways to get out. Put it over the green and you're in a gully with deep brush. So, too, the 190-yard par-3 seventh, the club's signature hole. With a 20-foot gully in front and behind the small, sloping green, and a large stand of white pines closing in on the right, even the best of golfers consider making par here as having done well. The back nine, which opened for play in 1998, was designed locally; it's tighter and a little longer than the front. The greens are larger with more noticeable breaks. The clubhouse is a former one-room schoolhouse.

COURSES NEARBY: Bethel Inn, Bridgton Highlands, Norway,

LAKEVIEW GOLF CLUB
PRAIRIE ROAD
BURNHAM
207-948-5414
REGION: Kennebec/Moose River Region
MAP: 21
ESTABLISHED: 1927
NUMBER OF HOLES: 9
COURSE LENGTH/PAR: Back: 6,032/72   **Middle:** 5,900/72   **Front:** 5,396/72
COURSE RATING/SLOPE: Back: 68.0/107 **Middle:** 68.0/107   **Front:** 69.9/114
HEAD PROFESSIONAL: No
COURSE ARCHITECT: Ronello Reynolds
GOLF FACILITIES: Full pro shop, club rental, cart rental, pull-cart rental, instruction, locker room, snack bar
TEE TIMES: Not necessary
RANGER: Yes
TIME TO PLAY 18 HOLES: 3 hours, 30 minutes
EARLIEST TEE-OFF: 7 a.m.
GREEN FEES: Weekend (18): $ Weekday (18): $
PAYMENT: Cash only

Season: April till snowfall

Local Chamber of Commerce: Mid-Maine, 207-873-3315 or 3316

Local Attractions: Unity Pond, fishing

Directions: From Waterville take I-95 to Exit 37. Turn right off the ramp onto Route 11/100. Take a left and travel about 6 miles to Burnham. Turn right onto Troy Road. Follow this for 4 miles. Turn right onto Prairie Road. The course is on your left.

Course Description: Designed and built by family patriarch Ronello Reynolds, Lakeside Golf Course has served the summer community and year-round residents near Unity Pond (known to locals as Lake Winnecook) for more than 70 years. Holes are generally straightaway, with level fairways and small greens. The first hole, a 387-yard dogleg left, has one of the prettiest green locations in Maine, sitting high on the pond's edge. At 514 yards, the par-5 sixth is not only the longest but also the toughest hole on the course. The ninth heads back toward the Reynolds family home, which sits on the hill to the right of the green. If you're wondering, yes, the large plate-glass window has needed to be replaced several times over the years. A friendly club with limited facilities.

Courses Nearby: Cedar Springs, Country View, J. W. Parks,

Lakewood Golf Club

Route 201

Lakewood Center

Madison

207-474-5955

Region: Kennebec/Moose River Region

Map: 20

Established: 1926

Number of Holes: 18

Course Length/Par: Back: 6,300/72   **Front:** 5,490/72

Course Rating/Slope: Back: 68.4/122 **Front:** 71.9/120

Head Professional: No

Course Architect: Alex Chisholm (O9), Philip Wogan (A9)

Golf Facilities: Full pro shop, practice green, practice bunker, club rental, club repair, club storage, cart rental, pull-cart rental, instruction, snack bar, lounge

Tee Times: Recommended

How Long in Advance: Unlimited

Ranger: Yes

Tee-Off Interval Time: 10 minutes

Time to Play 18 Holes: 4 hours

Earliest Tee-Off: 7 a.m.

Green Fees: Weekend (18): $$ Weekday (18): $

Payment: Cash only

Season: April through Thanksgiving

Local Chamber of Commerce: Madison-Anson, 207-696-3334

Local Attractions: Lakewood Theatre, Hayden Lake, white-water rafting

Directions: From Skowhegan drive 5 miles north on Route 201. The course is on your left, the clubhouse on your right.

Course Description: This course was built across the street from Lakewood Theatre and thrived at a time when summer productions included stars such as Humphrey Bogart, Tom Tempest, and Ginger Rogers. The layout has since expanded to 18 holes, and the club is now owned by the Browne family (see Natanis Golf Course). The front nine is of the old style, characterized by small greens and generous fairways. The newer back nine is tighter and features sloping fairways and rolling two-tiered greens. There are beautiful views of the Rangeley Mountains (including Bigelow and Sugarloaf) from the fourteenth green and fifteenth tee. As you would expect, this setting is spectacular in fall. As a nine-hole course, the signature hole was the 410-yard par-4 eighth. It's a downhill dogleg left; a pond stretches across the fairway just in front of the small back to front sloping green. Today most players talk about the 660-yard (700 yards from the tips) par-6 twelfth, the only par-6 in the state. Despite its length, locals claim it's a good birdie hole, provided your tee shot reaches the first plateau on this dogleg right. Mere mortals will likely have a blind second shot toward two ponds that lie at right angles to each other.

Courses Nearby: Loons Cove, Sugarloaf/USA

The Ledges Golf Club
One Ledges Drive
York
207-351-3000
Web: www.ledgesgolf.com
Region: Southern Coast
Map: 1
Established: 1998
Number of Holes: 18
Course Length/Par: Back: 6,978/72 **Middle:** 6,357/72 **Front:** 4,997/72
Course Rating/Slope: Back: 74.4/144 **Middle:** 71.2/135 **Front:** 65.6/129
Head Professional: Yes
Course Architect: William Bradley Booth
Golf Facilities: Full pro shop, driving range, practice green, practice bunker, club rental, club repair, cart rental, pull-cart rental, instruction, restaurant
Tee Times: Recommended
How Long in Advance: 4 days
Ranger: Yes
Tee-Off Interval Time: 8 minutes
Time to Play 18 Holes: 4 hours, 15 minutes

EARLIEST TEE-OFF: 7 a.m.

GREEN FEES: Weekend (18): $$$$ Weekday (18): $$$$

PAYMENT: MasterCard, Visa, American Express

SEASON: April through October

LOCAL CHAMBER OF COMMERCE: The Yorks, 207-363-4422

LOCAL ATTRACTIONS: The Yorks, historical sites, beaches

DIRECTIONS: Take Exit 4 off the Maine Turnpike (I-95). Turn right off the ramp, then south onto Route 1. After 3/4 mile take a right onto Route 91. Ledges Drive is about 5 miles ahead on your right. The club is on the right.

COURSE DESCRIPTION: Less than two hours from Boston, The Ledges opened for play in June 1999 to good reviews. Designed by Ogunquit-based designer W. Bradley Booth—whose Maine work includes The Meadows (Litchfield) and Spring Meadows (Gray)—the 6,357-yard course features wide fairways and ample driving room. Greens are large (averaging 7,000 square feet) and undulating. Built on a 260-acre piece of property, the course crosses fairly hilly, tree-lined terrain, which adds to its beauty. From the highest points, the seventh, thirteenth, and seventeenth holes, three bridges in Portsmouth, New Hampshire, that span the Piscataqua River into Maine are visible. There are four sets of tees; elevation plays a role on several holes. From its tee 50 feet above the green, the 196-yard par-3 eighth plays shorter than the scorecard indicates but is complicated by water that nearly surrounds the 10,000-square-foot green, the largest on the course. On the other hand, the 547-yard par-5 eighteenth stretches to 618 yards from the back tees. Regardless of starting point, most golfers will have to lay up in front of a wetland that crosses the fairway leaving a 160- to 175-yard uphill approach. The modern clubhouse has a comfortable informal dining area, full pro shop, and large porch overlooking the course. The Ledges is sure to be ranked one of the top courses in Maine.

COURSES NEARBY: Cape Neddick, Highland Links, Links at Outlook, Sanford

LIMESTONE COUNTRY CLUB

SAWYER ROAD

LIMESTONE

207-328-7277

WEB: www.mainerec.com/lcc.html

REGION: Aroostook

MAP: 65

ESTABLISHED: 1961

NUMBER OF HOLES: 9

COURSE LENGTH/PAR: Back: 6,735/72   **Front:** 5,740/72

COURSE RATING/SLOPE: Back: 70.4/114 **Front:** NA

HEAD PROFESSIONAL: No

COURSE ARCHITECT: William Mitchell

GOLF FACILITIES: Full pro shop, driving range, practice green, practice bunker, club rental, club repair, cart rental, pull-cart rental, instruction, locker room, snack bar, lounge

TEE TIMES: Not necessary

RANGER: Yes

TIME TO PLAY 18 HOLES: 4 hours

EARLIEST TEE-OFF: 7 a.m.

GREEN FEES: Weekend (18): $ Weekday (18): $

PAYMENT: MasterCard, Visa, American Express

SEASON: April through October

LOCAL CHAMBER OF COMMERCE: Limestone, 207-325-4025

LOCAL ATTRACTIONS: Area potato festivals, Fort Fairfield block house

DIRECTIONS: Take I-95 to Houlton. Follow Route 1 North to Caribou and turn right onto Route 89, then left onto Sawyer Road. The course is about 1 mile ahead on your right.

COURSE DESCRIPTION: A 9-hole layout with 18 tees, Limestone's back nine is the second longest in Maine (Bucksport Golf Course takes top honors). Designed by William Mitchell in 1958, it was originally built as the base course (called Inland Winds) for the Loring Air Force Base. The airfield has since closed, and the course is now under private ownership. During its air force days, maintenance of the course was dependent on whether or not the base commander was a golfer or tennis player. No question now, as the new management has done a great job putting the course in shape. Relatively flat, fairways are well defined by trees, bunkers, and the occasional water hazard. Typical is the 525-yard par-5 second. Thick woods line either side of the fairway, tightening the approach to the green.

COURSES NEARBY: Aroostook Valley, Caribou, Limestone, Presque Isle

LINKS AT OUTLOOK

ROUTE 4

BERWICK

207-384-4653

REGION: Southern Coast

MAP: 2

ESTABLISHED: 1999

NUMBER OF HOLES: 18 (opening spring 2000)

COURSE LENGTH/PAR: Back: 6,508/71 **Middle:** 6,004/71 **Front:** 5,025/71

COURSE RATING/SLOPE: Back: 69.3/128 **Middle:** 67.3/122 **Front:** NA

HEAD PROFESSIONAL: Yes

COURSE ARCHITECT: Brian Silva

GOLF FACILITIES: Full pro shop, driving range, practice green, club rental, cart rental, pull-cart rental, snack bar

TEE TIMES: NA

RANGER: No

TIME TO PLAY 18 HOLES: 4 hours, 15 minutes

EARLIEST TEE-OFF: 7:00 a.m.

GREEN FEES: Weekend (18): $$$$ Weekday (18): $$$

PAYMENT: NA

SEASON: April 1 through November 1

LOCAL CHAMBER OF COMMERCE: Sanford/Springvale, 207-324-4280

LOCAL ATTRACTIONS: Historical sites, beaches

DIRECTIONS: From I-95 North take Exit 3, South Berwick. At the end of the ramp take a right onto Route 236. Follow for approximately 11 miles into South Berwick. Turn right onto Route 4. The course will be ½ mile on your right.

COURSE DESCRIPTION: Due to open in spring 2000, this newest of southern Maine courses is being heralded as "a links course in the true Scottish tradition." Except for its inland location, it certainly looks the part. Rolling farmland accentuates this unique layout that was designed by *Golf World*'s 1999 Architect of the Year. The course features few trees but lots of mounds, bunkers and substantial rough. The back nine traverses a large hill adding to its challenge.

COURSES NEARBY: Cape Neddick, Highland Links, The Ledges, Sanford

LOONS COVE GOLF COURSE

ROUTE 201

SKOWHEGAN

207-474-9550

REGION: Kennebec/Moose River Region

MAP: 21

ESTABLISHED: 1987

NUMBER OF HOLES: 9

COURSE LENGTH/PAR: Back: 2,250/54

COURSE RATING/SLOPE: Back: NA

HEAD PROFESSIONAL: No

COURSE ARCHITECT: Reggie Perkins; Denise and Vurle Jones

GOLF FACILITIES: Full pro shop, driving range, practice green, club rental, club repair, club storage, cart rental, pull-cart rental, snack bar, lounge

TEE TIMES: Not necessary

RANGER: No

TIME TO PLAY 18 HOLES: 2 hours, 30 minutes

EARLIEST TEE-OFF: 7:30 a.m.

GREEN FEES: Weekend (18): $ Weekday (18): $

PAYMENT: Cash only

SEASON: April 1 through November 1

LOCAL CHAMBER OF COMMERCE: Skowhegan Area, 207-474-3621

LOCAL ATTRACTIONS: White-water rafting, St. George State Park, fishing

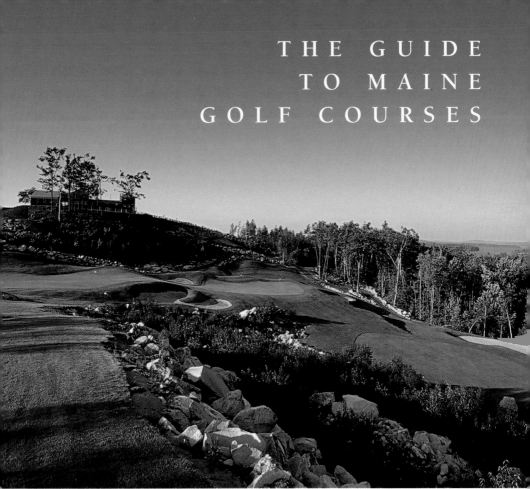

THE GUIDE
TO MAINE
GOLF COURSES

The view from the eighteenth fairway at Belgrade Lakes Golf Club looking toward the large green complex it shares with the ninth. Some of the 200,000 tons of rock moved during the course's construction divide the parallel fairways. Inset, Kebo Valley's clubhouse.

With more than 125 public access courses in the state, Maine is the best kept golfing secret in the Northeast. From small seaside tracks to majestic mountaintop layouts, you won't find more diversity, nor better quality anywhere in New England. Over the past 100 years such noted architects as H.C. Leeds, Willie Park, Jr., Donald Ross, and more recently Robert Trent Jones, Jr. and Dan Maples, among others, have contributed to the Maine golf landscape. History, beauty, challenge, it's all here for you to enjoy.

The 401-yard seventh at Indian Territory (top), Natanis Golf Club's award winning-layout. Built on former farm land, Arrowhead (below), Natanis' original nine, is a more open track. The Natanis clubhouse (inset) was built in 1995.

From the generous landing area on the par-4 tenth hole at Belgrade Lakes (top) it's an uphill approach to a sloped green with bunkers front and right. Three bunkers (known locally as the "Trio of Nasties") guard the left side of the fairway on the 375-yard fourth hole (left).

SUGARLOAF/USA, MICHAEL SCHROEDER (BOTTOM)

The signature 216-yard par-3
eleventh (left) is part of a six hole
stretch that makes up Sugarloaf/USA's
noted "String of Pearls."
The Carrabassett River (above)
meanders through these holes, never
more dramatically than at the dogleg
370-yard fourteenth (below).

Picture perfect is an apt description of the Bethel Inn & Country Club's 6,330-yard layout that traverses the foothills of the nearby White Mountains. Supporting that claim, the 522-yard par-5 fifth (far left) and the 410-yard fifteenth (below). The ninth green sits in the shadow of the historic Bethel Inn (left).

KEBO VALLEY CLUB.

Local Golf Rules
and Regulations
and Club Dues.
1899.

MICHAEL SCHROEDER

Small greens, man-made mounds and
cross bunkers add to Kebo Valley's vintage charm (left). The 413-yard eighth,
a hole Walter Hagen described as one of
the best par-4s he ever played (above).

MICHAEL SCHROEDER

FAR AND SURE

Grindstone Neck's 320-yard dogleg left
third hole (below) plays from an oceanside
tee to this small green set literally on the
edge of the sea. The ocean is visible from
every hole on the course.

Renowned golf course architect Donald Ross (left) had his hand in a number of Maine designs including Northeast Harbor Golf Club. Noted for its short but challenging par 4s, Northeast Harbor's 284-yard seventh (above) carves its way through thick spruce forest. Its right to left sloping fairway, narrow landing area and small target green put a premium on accuracy.

Dunegrass

Water is the obvious hazard at 197-yard seventeenth at Dunegrass Golf Club (left) designed by North Carolina-based Dan Maples. A new clubhouse (inset) provides ample room to relax following a round.

Dunegrass Golf Club (Left and top), Michael Schroeder (bottom)

Nonesuch River Golf Club

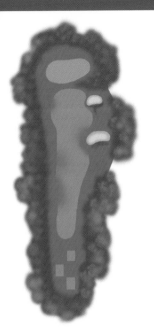

The 300-room Poland Spring House (above) reached its heyday during the early 1900s. Although the hotel no longer exists, a sporty 18-hole course designed by Donald Ross (fourth hole diagram left) still does. Another vintage resort is the Sebasco Harbor Resort (right) whose nine-hole oceanside track is undergoing renovations with plans to expand it to eighteen.

Southern Maine has seen a boom in golf course construction. Two notables are South Portland's Sable Oaks (below), which opened in 1989, and Nonesuch River (above) in Scarborough, which made its debut in 1998.

Although most of the Samoset Resort's golf holes have views of the water a few, including the 110-yard eleventh (above), cut through woods.

Penobscot Valley Country Club's brochure c. 1926 (left). President Howard Taft (right) once took 23 shots to get out of a now infamous bunker on the seventeenth hole at Kebo Valley. View from the tee at the 197-yard eighth hole at The Ledges Golf Club (below).

The view looking across the sixth green (and third hole) at the
Samoset Resort. Fourteen holes border on or look out over
Penobscot Bay and its islands.

The shingle-style clubhouse at Sable Oaks Golf Club has undergone recent renovations.

MICHAEL SCHROEDER

SABLE OAKS · GOLF CLUB

MICHAEL SCHROEDER

Jackson Brook crisscrosses the fairway of Sable Oaks' signature 480-yard par-5 fourteenth (diagram and left). It makes its first crossing about 250 yards out from the tee before winding its way back along the front and right of the green.

Risk, reward and nerves of steel are hallmarks of Sable Oaks' challenging 6,359 yard layout. Fairways are narrow, greens are big, fast and sloping, and bunkers are plentiful. Most holes leave little margin for error.

PARK MORRISON

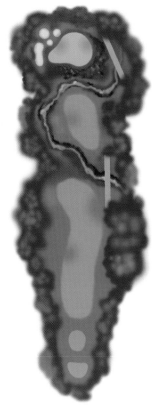

MICHAEL SCHROEDER, BELGRADE LAKES GOLF CLUB (BOTTOM)

KEVIN SHIELDS

SANFORD COUNTRY CLUB

A few of Maine's hidden gems — from the top — Poland Springs Golf Club; Blink Bonnie Golf Club and Sanford Country Club.

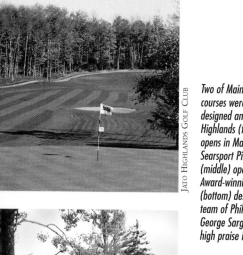

Two of Maine's newest golf courses were locally designed and built: Jato Highlands (top) in Lincoln opens in May 2000 and Searsport Pines in Searsport (middle) opened in 1999. Award-winning Point Sebago (bottom) designed by the team of Phil Wogan and George Sargent opened to high praise in 1996.

The historic mile-long Rockland Breakwater provides a spectacular backdrop
for the Samoset Resort's signature hole, the 481-yard fourth (below) — one of
several seaside holes that inspired the nickname, "Pebble Beach of the East."

Bunkers flank the fairway
on the 380-yard sixth hole
at the Samoset Resort. The
approach is uphill to a large
well-guarded green.

L.C. LAMBRECHT

The 181-yard eighth hole at Point Sebago (top) is typical of the course's par 3s: ample greens guarded by plenty of sand. The 290-yard, par-4 seventh hole at St. Croix Country Club (bottom), the easternmost golf course in the United States.

USGA/JOHN MUMMERT, POINT SEBAGO RESORT (TOP)

DIRECTIONS: Take Exit 36 off I-95, then Route 201 North. The course is about 10 miles ahead on your right.

COURSE DESCRIPTION: Pretty Kennebec River views from this par-3 course. Loons Cove comes into play on several holes, the longest of which is 185 yards. New owners have added bunkers and are rebuilding some greens and tees. Lots of wildlife: beavers, muskrats, ducks, geese and, of course, loons.

COURSES NEARBY: Lakewood

LUCERNE-IN-MAINE GOLF COURSE
ROUTE 1A
LUCERNE-IN-MAINE
207-843-6282

REGION: Acadia/Down East

MAP: 23

ESTABLISHED: 1926

NUMBER OF HOLES: 9 (expanding to 18)

COURSE LENGTH/PAR: Back: 6,410/72   **Middle:** 5,760/72   **Front:** 5,300/72

COURSE RATING/SLOPE: Back: 70.6/119 **Middle:** 67.4/119   **Front:** 69.5/116

HEAD PROFESSIONAL: Yes

COURSE ARCHITECT: Donald Ross

GOLF FACILITIES: Full pro shop, driving range, practice green, practice bunker, club rental, club repair, club storage, cart rental, pull-cart rental, instruction, restaurant, lounge

TEE TIMES: Recommended

RANGER: Yes

TEE-OFF INTERVAL TIME: 8 minutes

TIME TO PLAY 18 HOLES: 4 hours, 30 minutes

EARLIEST TEE-OFF: 7 a.m.

GREEN FEES: Weekend (18): $$ Weekday (18): $$

PAYMENT: MasterCard, Visa

SEASON: Mid-April through October

LOCAL CHAMBER OF COMMERCE: Bangor Region, 207-947-0307

LOCAL ATTRACTIONS: Phipps Lake, hiking, Greater Bangor area

DIRECTIONS: From I-95 in Bangor take Exit 45 to Route 395 and on to Route 1A. Turn right on Route 1A and drive about 8 miles. The course is on your left. (From Ellsworth it's 14 miles north on Route 1A.)

COURSE DESCRIPTION: This Donald Ross–designed course was reclaimed in 1993 after having been abandoned and overgrown since 1979. Originally part of Lucerne Inn Resort, the club now operates as an independent entity. While the routing is the same, the number sequence is new. This is a typical Donald Ross layout: tree-lined fairways with ample landing areas and small greens (3,000 square feet) guarded by pot bunkers. Its hilly nature favors a pitch-and-run approach to most greens. You'll remember the 350 yard fifth, a classic dogleg left with a severely rolling fairway leading to a small, sloped green. The 485-yard par-5 eighth is all uphill and further complicated by the fact that the fairway slopes right to left. The driving range that borders it to the right is out of bounds. The course plays on both sides of Route 1A, a complication the new owners (as of 1999) plan to alleviate with a tunnel underneath the busy road. Also in the works is an expanded clubhouse and plans to add nine new holes. The hillside setting provides spectacular views overlooking the historic Lucerne Inn, Phipps Lake and Bald Mountain.

COURSES NEARBY: Bangor Municipal, Bucksport, Felt Brook, White Birches

MAPLE LANE INN & GOLF CLUB
295 MAPLE LANE
LIVERMORE FALLS
207-897-6666
WEB: www.livfalls.com/mapleln.html
REGION: Western Lakes and Mountains
MAP: 11
ESTABLISHED: 1978
NUMBER OF HOLES: 9
COURSE LENGTH/PAR: Back: 6,038/70   **Middle:** 5,600/70   **Front:** 5,330/70
COURSE RATING/SLOPE: Back: 65.0/118 **Middle:** 62.8/114   **Front:** 65.8/118
HEAD PROFESSIONAL: Yes
COURSE ARCHITECT: Dennis R. Grasso
GOLF FACILITIES: Full pro shop, practice green, practice bunker, club rental, cart rental, pull-cart rental, instruction, restaurant, lounge, accommodations
TEE TIMES: Not necessary
RANGER: No
TIME TO PLAY 18 HOLES: 3 hours, 45 minutes
EARLIEST TEE-OFF: Dawn
GREEN FEES: Weekend (18): $ Weekday (18): $
PAYMENT: All major credit cards
SEASON: April 1 through November 1
LOCAL CHAMBER OF COMMERCE: Jay, Livermore, Livermore Falls, 207-897-6755
LOCAL ATTRACTIONS: Lakes, Androscoggin River
DIRECTIONS: From Portland take the Maine Turnpike to Exit 12. Follow Route 4 North for 28 miles to Livermore Falls. Take a right onto River Road (just before the river). The inn and course are 5 miles ahead.
COURSE DESCRIPTION: The Maple Lane Inn was originally a tavern and inn built in 1790 to serve travelers along the stagecoach line from Farmington to Portland. The building was relocated to River Road and now serves as a six-room B&B that nicely complements this well-maintained nine-hole track. Broad tree-lined fairways make this a fair but challenging test. All the par-3s here are tough, particu-

larly the 155-yard fifth. From an elevated tee you must hit to a small green with a pond running along its front side. The rebuilt 555-yard third is one of two long par-5s and requires a 180-yard drive to clear water off the tee. Stay-and-play packages are available.

COURSES NEARBY: Oakdale, Turner Highlands, Wilson Lake

MARS HILL COUNTRY CLUB

YORK ROAD
MARS HILL
207-425-4802
WEB: www.mainerec.com/mhcc
REGION: Aroostook
MAP: 59
ESTABLISHED: 1991
NUMBER OF HOLES: 9 (expanding to 18)
COURSE LENGTH/PAR: Back: 6,286/72   **Middle:** 5,940/72   **Front:** 5,384/72
COURSE RATING/SLOPE: Back: NA   **Middle:** 68.8/120   **Front:** NA
HEAD PROFESSIONAL: No
COURSE ARCHITECT: Alton McQuade
GOLF FACILITIES: Full pro shop, driving range, practice green, practice bunker, club rental, club storage, cart rental, pull-cart rental, showers, restaurant, lounge
TEE TIMES: Not necessary
RANGER: Yes
TIME TO PLAY 18 HOLES: 4 hours
EARLIEST TEE-OFF: 7 a.m.
GREEN FEES: Weekend (18): $ Weekday (18): $
PAYMENT: MasterCard, Visa
SEASON: Late April through October
LOCAL CHAMBER OF COMMERCE: Presque Isle Area, 207-764-6561
LOCAL ATTRACTIONS: Mars Hill, hiking
DIRECTIONS: From Bangor take I-95 to Houlton, then take Route 1 North about 25 miles to Route 1A in Mars Hill. Follow Route 1A for few hundred yards, then turn right onto Boynton Road and follow to its end. Turn left onto York Road. The course is on your right.
COURSE DESCRIPTION: The village of Mars Hill is dominated by the 1,700-foot hill of the same name. Traversing the mountain's lower reaches is the Mars Hill Country Club. Designed and built in 1991 by former contractor Alton McQuade, Mars Hill is regarded as one of the finest nine-hole courses in Aroostook County. Popular among locals, it also draws a regular Canadian contingent from nearby New Brunswick. Even though most holes are straightway, the 6,286-yard layout takes advantage of its hilly locale and presents a good test for all levels. The memorable 470-yard par-5 third, for example, drops dramatically off the tee. The elevation will help your tee shot, which needs to clear a watery ravine about 180

yards out. But the approach, no matter how big a hitter you are, will be uphill to a back-to-front-sloping green. Mars Hill is well maintained. Few changes have been made to the original layout, but lessons learned over the past nine years will be incorporated into a new nine—also designed by Alton McQuade—scheduled to open in 2000.

COURSES NEARBY: Aroostook Valley, Caribou, Houlton Community, Limestone, Presque Isle,

THE MEADOWS GOLF CLUB
HUNTINGTON HILL ROAD
LITCHFIELD
207-268-3000

REGION: Kennebec/Moose River Region

MAP: 12

ESTABLISHED: 1998

NUMBER OF HOLES: 18

COURSE LENGTH/PAR: Back: 5,845/68   **Middle:** 5,634/68   **Front:** 4,505/68

COURSE RATING/SLOPE: Back: 68.6/126   **Middle:** 66.2/121   **Front:** 66.0/117

HEAD PROFESSIONAL: No

COURSE ARCHITECT: William Bradley Booth

GOLF FACILITIES: Practice green, club rental, club repair, cart rental, pull-cart rental, snack bar, lounge

TEE TIMES: Recommended weekends and holidays

HOW LONG IN ADVANCE: 1 week

RANGER: Yes

TEE-OFF INTERVAL TIME: 9 minutes

TIME TO PLAY 18 HOLES: 4 hours

EARLIEST TEE-OFF: 6:30 a.m.

GREEN FEES: Weekend (18): $$ **Weekday (18):** $$

PAYMENT: MasterCard, Visa

SEASON: Late April through early November

LOCAL CHAMBER OF COMMERCE: Kennebec Valley, 207-623-4559

LOCAL ATTRACTIONS: Greater Augusta, Lewiston-Auburn, Cobbossee Lake

DIRECTIONS: From Exit 26 off I-95 turn left onto Route 197. Travel about 7 miles to Huntington Road, on your right. The course is on the left.

COURSE DESCRIPTION: Just 20 minutes from Lewiston and Augusta, this is Ogunquit-based designer Brad Booth's first full 18-hole Maine design (see The Ledges Golf Club). And it is impressive for a number of reasons. Built on just 112 acres with wetlands throughout the site, it was obviously a tough assignment. The course is short only because it features six par-3s. A scenic layout, each nine plays downhill into a valley then returns to finish at the clubhouse. Every hole is tree lined and separate from other holes. Big, contoured greens offer good targets but tough putting. Four sets of tees make it playable for all levels.

Courses Nearby: Apple Valley, Cobbossee Colony, Kennebec Heights, Springbrook

Mere Creek Golf Course
551 Fitch Avenue
Brunswick
207-921-2155
Region: Mid-Coast Region
Map: 6
Established: 1958
Number of Holes: 9
Course Length/Par: Back: 6,284/72   **Front:** 5,594/74
Course Rating/Slope: Back: 68.9/119 **Front:** 71.4/119
Head Professional: Yes
Course Architect: Mark Verhey
Golf Facilities: Full pro shop, driving range, practice green, practice bunker, club rental, club storage, cart rental, pull-cart rental, instruction, locker room, showers, snack bar, lounge
Tee Times: Necessary on weekends
How Long in Advance: 1 week
Ranger: Yes
Tee-Off Interval Time: 8 minutes
Time to Play 18 Holes: 4 hours
Earliest Tee-Off: 7 a.m.
Green Fees: Weekend (18): $$ Weekday (18): $
Payment: MasterCard, Visa, American Express
Season: May 1 through November 15
Local Chamber of Commerce: Bath-Brunswick Region, 207-725-8797
Local Attractions: Bowdoin College, L. L. Bean (Freeport), air shows
Directions: From Portland take I-95 North to Exit 22. Follow Route 1 North to the Cook's Corner exit. Turn right onto Route 24, then left at the light to Brunswick Naval Air Station. Follow signs to the course.
Course Description: Located on the grounds of the Brunswick Naval Air Station and owned by the U.S. Navy, this course recently changed its name in an effort to encourage civilian play. It is one of several fine courses in the Brunswick area. Fairly open and flat, it is nonetheless a challenging layout. The 432-yard par-4 sixth is regarded locally as one of its best. Straightaway, it's tightly tree lined with fairway bunkers to the left. The green is typical of most on the course, small and sloping strongly back to front. Different tee boxes on the front and back often give new perspective to holes during your second loop. The 372-yard dogleg second, for example, shortens to 314 yards and straightens out, making it a little easier the second time through.
Courses Nearby: Bath, Brunswick, Freeport, Shore Acres

MINGO SPRINGS GOLF COURSE

MINGO LOOP ROAD
RANGELEY
207-864-5021
REGION: Western Lakes and Mountains
MAP: 28
ESTABLISHED: 1971
NUMBER OF HOLES: 18
COURSE LENGTH/PAR: Back: 6,300/70   **Front:** 6,000/70
COURSE RATING/SLOPE: Back: 66.3/109 **Front:** 67.4/110
HEAD PROFESSIONAL: Yes
COURSE ARCHITECT: Arthur Fenn, Eugene Wogan
GOLF FACILITIES: Full pro shop, driving range, practice green, club rental, club repair, club storage, cart rental, pull-cart rental, instruction, locker room, snack bar
TEE TIMES: Recommended
HOW LONG IN ADVANCE: 2 weeks
RANGER: Yes
TEE-OFF INTERVAL TIME: 7–8 minutes
TIME TO PLAY 18 HOLES: 3 hours, 20 minutes
EARLIEST TEE-OFF: 7 a.m.
GREEN FEES: Weekend (18): $$$ Weekday (18): $$$
PAYMENT: MasterCard, Visa
SEASON: Mid-May through September
LOCAL CHAMBER OF COMMERCE: Rangeley Lakes Region, 207-864-5364
LOCAL ATTRACTIONS: Rangeley Lakes
DIRECTIONS: From Auburn take Exit 12 off the Maine Turnpike (I-495). Follow Route 4 North through Farmington to Rangeley village, then travel approximately 2 miles toward Oquossoc. Take a left onto Mingo Loop Road. Follow signs to the course.
COURSE DESCRIPTION: Set high on hillside overlooking Rangeley Lake and Saddleback and Bald Mountains, Mingo Springs ranks as one of western Maine's most scenic layouts. Two separate nines built in the 1920s were combined into one 18-hole layout in 1972. Both sides maintain classic design touches, the first nine being noted for its elevated tees and greens and the inward nine as flatter and more links-style, favoring bump-and-run approaches. The well-bunkered greens are typically small and sloping with subtle undulations. A challenging and enjoyable course for the good golfer that is also, as one local put it, "beginner friendly."
COURSES NEARBY: Sugarloaf/USA

MOOSE RIVER GOLF CLUB
ROUTE 201
JACKMAN
207-668-4841
REGION: Kennebec/Moose River Region
MAP: 39
ESTABLISHED: 1935
NUMBER OF HOLES: 9
COURSE LENGTH/PAR: Back: 3,952/62
COURSE RATING/SLOPE: Back: NA
HEAD PROFESSIONAL: No
COURSE ARCHITECT: NA
GOLF FACILITIES: Practice green, club rental, club storage, cart rental, pull-cart rental, snacks
TEE TIMES: Not necessary
RANGER: No
TIME TO PLAY 18 HOLES: 2 hours, 30 minutes
EARLIEST TEE-OFF: 7 a.m.
GREEN FEES: Weekend (18): $ Weekday (18): $
PAYMENT: Cash only
SEASON: April through September
LOCAL CHAMBER OF COMMERCE: Jackman–Moose River Region, 207-668-4171
LOCAL ATTRACTIONS: White-water rafting, lakes, fishing
DIRECTIONS: From Exit 36 off I-95 take Route 201 to Jackman. The course is about 1 mile past Jackman on your right.
COURSE DESCRIPTION: About 10 miles from the Canadian border in northwest Maine, Moose River is a short layout that features narrow fairways and small, fairly flat greens. Despite its length, it offers its share of challenges. It is laid out along the side of a hill, so several holes play either uphill or downhill. A level lie is hard to come by. Water, too, is a factor on a few holes—in particular the 171-yard sixth, where a pond stretches in front of the postage-stamp green. And what about the old-time cemetery between the first and third greens? It's out of bounds. With mountains all around, this scenic course is a rural Maine treat.
COURSES NEARBY: Mount Kineo, Squaw Mountain

MOUNT KINEO GOLF COURSE
MOUNT KINEO ON MOOSEHEAD LAKE
ROCKWOOD
207-534-9012
REGION: Katahdin/Moosehead Region
MAP: 41

ESTABLISHED: Circa 1900

NUMBER OF HOLES: 9

COURSE LENGTH/PAR: Back: 6,022/72   **Front:** 5,562/72

COURSE RATING/SLOPE: Back: NA   **Front:** NA

HEAD PROFESSIONAL: No

COURSE ARCHITECT: Art Townley, Orrin Smith (R)

GOLF FACILITIES: Pro shop, club rental, club storage, cart rental, pull-cart rental, locker room, snack bar, lounge

TEE TIMES: Not necessary

RANGER: No

TIME TO PLAY 18 HOLES: 4 hours, 30 minutes

EARLIEST TEE-OFF: 8 a.m.

GREEN FEES: Weekend (18): $ Weekday (18): $

PAYMENT: MasterCard, Visa

SEASON: End of May through September

LOCAL CHAMBER OF COMMERCE: Moosehead Lake Region, 207-695-2702

LOCAL ATTRACTIONS: Moosehead Lake, hiking, fishing

DIRECTIONS: From Augusta take I-95 North to Exit 39 (Newport). Follow Route 7 North to Dexter. Take Route 23 to Guilford, then follow Route 15/6 to Greenville and Rockwood. A boat shuttle to Kineo leaves each hour.

COURSE DESCRIPTION: A remote peninsula in Moosehead Lake provides one of the more unusual golf settings in Maine. Built at the turn of the century as part of the Mt. Kineo House resort, a 500-room hotel that was owned and operated by the Rikker (later changed to Ricker) family of Poland Spring fame, the course is only accessible by boat. Flush up against the majestic 734-foot Mount Kineo, several of the current nine holes use the mountain as a backdrop. The signature hole, for example, is the 138-yard fourth. Playing over water, the small green tucks up against thick woods that gradually give way to steep granite cliffs. Views of Moosehead Lake—Maine's largest—are equally dramatic. Mount Kineo's other par-3, the 140-yard seventh, starts off from an elevated tee and has the lake to its right. Winds can make your tee shot tricky, since the small green sits just 15 yards from the water. The clubhouse is small with limited facilities, but there is an eight-room B&B on the peninsula. A boat leaves from Rockwood on the hour.

COURSES NEARBY: Moose River, Squaw Mountain Village

NAPLES GOLF CLUB
OLD ROUTE 114
NAPLES
207-693-6424

REGION: Western Lakes and Mountains

MAP: 4

ESTABLISHED: 1921

NUMBER OF HOLES: 9 (expanding to 18)

Course Length/Par: Back: 6,554/72 **Front:** 5,416/72
Course Rating/Slope: Back: 69.5/115 **Front:** NA
Head Professional: Yes
Course Architect: NA
Golf Facilities: Full pro shop, practice green, club rental, club repair, club storage, cart rental, pull-cart rental, instruction, snack bar, lounge
Tee Times: Not necessary
Ranger: Yes
Time to Play 18 Holes: 4 hours
Earliest Tee-Off: 6:30 a.m.
Green Fees: Weekend (18): $$ **Weekday (18): $$**
Payment: MasterCard, Visa
Season: April through October
Local Chamber of Commerce: Bridgton Lakes Region, 207-647-3472
Local Attractions: Sebago Lake, camping
Directions: From Portland take Exit 8 off the Maine Turnpike. Follow Route 302 for 30 miles to Route 114 and turn left. The course is on your left.
Course Description: In the heart of Maine's Sebago Lake area, Naples has long been a popular summer retreat. This locally designed nine-hole track plays along the hilly terrain bordering Brandy Pond (aka Bay of Naples). In fact, the green on the 425-yard par-4 fourth hole takes full advantage of its locale. Almost a double dogleg, it plays downhill to the right before bending slightly left with the green perched just shy of the water's edge. Blind approaches to small, fast, well-contoured greens make for plenty of challenge. A new nine is under construction and due to be completed by August 2000.
Courses Nearby: Allen Mountain, Bridgton Highlands, Frye Island, Point Sebago

Natanis Golf Club
Webber Pond Road
Vassalboro
207-622-3561
Region: Kennebec/Moose River Region
Map: 13
Established: 1965
Number of Holes: 27 (expanding to 36)
Course Length/Par: (Tomahawk and Indian Territory) Back: 6,667/72
Middle: 6,184/72   **Front:** 5,376/72/36
Course Rating/Slope
 (Tomahawk and Indian Territory): Back: 68.5/118   **Middle:** NA
Front: NA
Head Professional: Yes

COURSE ARCHITECT: Paul Browne, Ben Gray, Philip Wogan

GOLF FACILITIES: Full pro shop, driving range, practice green, practice bunker, club rental, club repair, club storage, cart rental, pull-cart rental, instruction, l ocker room, snack bar, lounge

TEE TIMES: Necessary on weekends and holidays

HOW LONG IN ADVANCE: 1 week

RANGER: Yes

TEE-OFF INTERVAL TIME: 8 minutes

TIME TO PLAY 18 HOLES: 4 hours, 15 minutes

EARLIEST TEE-OFF: 6 a.m. (depending on season)

GREEN FEES: **Weekend (18): $$**   **Weekday (18): $**

PAYMENT: MasterCard, Visa

SEASON: Early April through early November

LOCAL CHAMBER OF COMMERCE: Mid-Maine, 207-873-3315 or 3316

LOCAL ATTRACTIONS: Augusta area, China Lake

DIRECTIONS: From Augusta take Exit 30 off I-95. Turn right off the ramp onto Route 100/201 into Augusta. At the rotary(s) follow Route 201 North for 6 miles. Webber Road is on your right, and the course is about 2 miles ahead on your left.

COURSE DESCRIPTION: Just 20 minutes north of Augusta, Natanis is composed of three separate nine-hole courses: Arrowhead, Tomahawk, and Indian Territory. Two 9s are designated as the 18-hole "course of the day." Each course has its own distinct personality. Arrowhead, the oldest of the three, was built in 1965 on the site of a former dairy farm. It has wide-open holes with large greens (several of which were originally designed in the shape of Maine counties). The Tomahawk course is longer and tighter. At 600 yards, the par-5 fourth is the longest on all three courses. A good tee shot is required on the 335-yard sixth due to the traversing water hazard approximately 160 yards out. Natanis's signature nine is the Phil Wogan–designed Indian Territory, ranked by *Golf Digest* as one of the top nine-hole courses in Maine and one of the top 500 public courses in the United States. Sculpted out of thick Maine woods, Indian is characterized by narrow fairways and peppered with bunkers and several water hazards. The signature par-3 third hole features a 60-foot drop in elevation, tee to green, with water circling the entire right side and bunkers left. Water also comes into play on both your tee shot and approach on the 480-yard par-5 fifth. The uphill approach to a steeply elevated green makes the seemingly short 385-yard eighth hole into a par-5. Save this hole for late afternoon and you'll be rewarded with a beautiful view back through the tree-lined fairway toward the setting sun. A 3,000-square-foot clubhouse, built in 1995, with wraparound porch complements the golf experience. Work is under way to incorporate an additional Dan Maples–designed nine for a total of 36 holes by year 2001.

COURSES NEARBY: Belgrade Lakes, Capitol City, Cedar Springs, Kennebec Heights, Pine Ridge, Western View, Waterville

NONESUCH RIVER GOLF CLUB

304 GORHAM ROAD
SCARBOROUGH
207-883-0007
WEB: www.megolf.com
REGION: Greater Portland Area
MAP: 3
ESTABLISHED: 1997
NUMBER OF HOLES: 18
COURSE LENGTH/PAR: Back: 6,218/70   **Middle:** 5,691/70   **Front:** 5,032/70
COURSE RATING/SLOPE: Back: 68.8/119 **Middle:** 66.9/116   **Front:** 68.8/109
HEAD PROFESSIONAL: Yes
COURSE ARCHITECT: Tom Walker
GOLF FACILITIES: Full pro shop, driving range, practice green, practice bunker, club rental, club repair, club storage, cart rental, pull-cart rental, instruction, snack bar, lounge
TEE TIMES: Recommended
HOW LONG IN ADVANCE: 7 days
RANGER: Yes
TEE-OFF INTERVAL TIME: 8 minutes
TIME TO PLAY 18 HOLES: 4 hours, 15 minutes
EARLIEST TEE-OFF: 6 a.m. weekend, 6:30 a.m. weekday
GREEN FEES: Weekend (18): $$$ **Weekday (18): $$**
PAYMENT: MasterCard, Visa
SEASON: April 15 through November 30
LOCAL CHAMBER OF COMMERCE: Greater Portland Region, 207-772-2811
LOCAL ATTRACTIONS: Maine Mall, Portland Sea Dogs, Greater Portland area, beaches
DIRECTIONS: From Exit 6 off the Maine Turnpike (I-95) turn left onto Payne Road. After about 1 mile take a left onto Route 114 (Gorham Road). Go over the turnpike. The course is the first left.
COURSE DESCRIPTION: Formerly the site of the Greens at Eaglebrook, Nonesuch River was completely redesigned and expanded to 18 holes in 1997. Minutes from the Maine Mall and Maine Turnpike, its location is ideal for visitors to the Portland area. A fairly level layout, most of the new holes cut through woods. With four tees and generous landing areas, the course is playable for all levels. Good course management is necessary, however, as wetlands cut across or encroach fairways on several holes. The 496-yard par-5 third is a good example. A long hitter will have to lay up in front of water that cuts across the fairway. More water on the right and trees will likely make you think twice about the long approach into a narrow green. The thirteenth, a dogleg left of 374 yards, has similar wetland hazards and an elevated green beautifully framed by tall trees. The course is noted for its well-maintained greens. Comfortable and accommodating modern clubhouse.

COURSES NEARBY: Biddeford-Saco, Dunegrass, Dutch Elm, Gorham, Old Orchard Beach, Pleasant Hill, Riverside, Sable Oaks, Salmon Falls, South Portland Municipal, Willowdale

NORTH HAVEN GOLF CLUB
IRON POINT ROAD
NORTH HAVEN
207-867-2054
REGION: Mid-Coast Region
MAP: 15
ESTABLISHED: Circa 1930
NUMBER OF HOLES: 9
COURSE LENGTH/PAR: Back: 6,080/70
COURSE RATING/SLOPE: Back: 68.4/112
HEAD PROFESSIONAL: No
COURSE ARCHITECT: Stiles & Van Kleek
GOLF FACILITIES: Club rental, club repair, club storage, cart rental, pull-cart rental
TEE TIMES: Not necessary
RANGER: No
TIME TO PLAY 18 HOLES: 2 hours, 30 minutes
EARLIEST TEE-OFF: 7 a.m.
GREEN FEES: Weekend (18): $$$ Weekday (18): $$$
PAYMENT: Cash only
SEASON: May through late October
LOCAL CHAMBER OF COMMERCE: Rockland-Thomaston Area, 207-596-0376
LOCAL ATTRACTIONS: Lobster Festival (Rockland), windjammers, boat excursions
DIRECTIONS: From Portland take I-95 to Exit 22 (Brunswick). Follow Route 1 to Rockland and from there take the North Haven ferry to North Haven. The course is an easy 1/4-mile walk (third left) from the North Haven ferry dock.
COURSE DESCRIPTION: A classic nine-hole track built for the summer community on this island in Penobscot Bay. Designed by the team of Wayne Stiles and John Van Kleek, it is little changed from its original layout. It is accessible by car ferry from Rockland. During the busy summer season, it is sometimes easier to leave your car on the Rockland side and make the short walk to the course from the island's terminal. As would be expected, this is a picturesque layout with numerous views of the water. The view from the seaside third green is virtually of the whole island. Most holes are straightaway and play back and forth along a gentle hillside. The 420-yard fourth, however, is a strong dogleg left that requires a big drive before you can even see the green. Wind is generally a factor here and can either help or hinder your play. Velvet bentgrass greens are not particularly fast but very well maintained. There are no public accommodations on the island, so you need to be aware of the ferry schedule.
COURSES NEARBY: Rockland, Samoset Resort

NORTHEAST HARBOR GOLF CLUB
SARGENT DRIVE
NORTHEAST HARBOR
207-276-5335
REGION: Acadia/Down East
MAP: 16
ESTABLISHED: 1895
NUMBER OF HOLES: 18
COURSE LENGTH/PAR: Back: 5,430/69 **Middle:** 5,278/69 **Front:** 4,530/71
COURSE RATING/SLOPE: Back: 67.8/120 **Middle:** 66.7/118 **Front:** 67.3/116
HEAD PROFESSIONAL: Yes
COURSE ARCHITECT: J. G. Thorp, Donald Ross, Herbert Strong (A9)
GOLF FACILITIES: Full pro shop, practice green, club rental, club repair, club storage, cart rental, pull-cart rental, instruction, locker room
TEE TIMES: Not necessary
RANGER: No
TIME TO PLAY 18 HOLES: 4 hours, 15 minutes
EARLIEST TEE-OFF: 7 a.m.
GREEN FEES: Weekend (18): $$$$ **Weekday (18):** $$$$
PAYMENT: MasterCard, Visa
SEASON: Memorial Day through Labor Day
LOCAL CHAMBER OF COMMERCE: Mount Desert, 207-244-7312
LOCAL ATTRACTIONS: Acadia National Park, Somes Sound, Bar Harbor, shopping
DIRECTIONS: From Ellsworth take Route 3 to Mount Desert Island, then take Route 198 from the head of the island to Somesville. Take a left at the traffic light (following Route 198) and proceed 3 miles to Sargent Drive. Turn right. The course is 2 miles ahead on your left.

COURSE DESCRIPTION: Another of Maine's turn-of-the-century classics, Northeast Harbor Golf Club on Mount Desert Island is located on the east side of Somes Sound, the only fjord on the East Coast. The original layout, designed in 1895 by J. G. Thorp, was located across the street from its present site. Although not documented, oral history suggests that Donald Ross designed the first nine holes (presently 1–6 and 13–15) when the club relocated to the east side of Sargent Drive in 1919. Herbert Strong, designer of two U.S. Open venues, laid out a second nine (today's 7–12 and 16–18), which was opened in 1925. Measuring just 5,430 yards, Northeast is noted for its very small, meticulously maintained greens. A good short game is important here. Most memorable of Northeast Harbor's classic short par-4s are the 325-yard fifth and the 335-yard seventh. A gully cuts across the fairway on five about 100 yards out from the elevated green. A large cedar tree hampers approaches coming from the hole's right side. Position here is key. The seventh also requires accuracy off the tee. Trees encroach on the right side of this narrow right-to-left-sloping fairway and block your view of the green. A good drive is rewarded. Typical among this venue's par-3s is the 149-yard par-3 third. From the elevated tee to the elevated green there's nothing but trouble. Leave your tee shot short and you're facing a steep uphill chip. Hit it long and you'll disappear into the thick spruce forest that's ever present for the next 15 holes.

COURSES NEARBY: Bar Harbor, Causeway, Kebo Valley

NORTHPORT GOLF CLUB
BLUFF ROAD
NORTHPORT
207-338-2270
REGION: Mid-Coast Region
MAP: 14
ESTABLISHED: 1916
NUMBER OF HOLES: 9
COURSE LENGTH/PAR: Back: 6,087/72   **Front:** 5,444/74
COURSE RATING/SLOPE: Back: 68.0/112 **Front:** 71.4/113
HEAD PROFESSIONAL: Yes
COURSE ARCHITECT: George Jennings
GOLF FACILITIES: Full pro shop, driving range, practice green, club rental, cart rental, pull-cart rental, instruction, snack bar
TEE TIMES: Not necessary
RANGER: Yes
TIME TO PLAY 18 HOLES: 4 hours
EARLIEST TEE-OFF: 7 a.m.
GREEN FEES: Weekend (18): $$ **Weekday (18): $$**
PAYMENT: MasterCard, Visa
SEASON: April 15 through October 31
LOCAL CHAMBER OF COMMERCE: Belfast Area, 207-338-5900
LOCAL ATTRACTIONS: Greater Belfast, Camden area, Penobscot Bay
DIRECTIONS: From Brunswick take Route 1 North through Camden. About 10 miles north of Camden take a right onto Shore Road. Bear right at a fork. The course is on your right.
COURSE DESCRIPTION: Built in 1916, Northport is a classically designed nine-hole layout. Except for its elevated tee on number one, the course is level and easy to walk, making it popular with seniors and beginners alike. Known for smooth greens, it is wide open with relatively few hazards. You will have to clear a pond on your approach to the 310-yard par-4 fourth, and a few bunkers guard the elevated, tiered green on the long 530-yard seventh. A small stream cuts across the corner of the 338-yard dogleg-right eighth hole. A large, Victorian-style clubhouse offers simple yet elegant comfort reminiscent of times gone by.
COURSES NEARBY: Country View, Goose River, Searsport Pines

Norway Country Club

Lake Road, Route 118
Norway
207-743-9840
Region: Western Lakes and Mountains
Map: 11
Established: 1929
Number of Holes: 9
Course Length/Par: Back: 5,818/70   **Middle:** 5,724/70   **Front:** 4,878/72
Course Rating/Slope: Back: NA   **Middle:** 66.6/107   **Front:** 65.9/103
Head Professional: Yes
Course Architect: George Dunn
Golf Facilities: Full pro shop, driving range, practice green, practice bunker, club rental, club repair, cart rental, pull-cart rental, instruction, locker room, restaurant, lounge
Tee Times: Not necessary
Ranger: Yes
Time to Play 18 Holes: 4 hours
Earliest Tee-Off: 7 a.m.
Green Fees: Weekend (18): $$ **Weekday (18): $$**
Payment: Cash only
Season: Mid-April through mid-October
Local Chamber of Commerce: Oxford Hills, 207-743-2281
Local Attractions: Lakes, hiking, camping
Directions: From Portland take Exit 11 off the Maine Turnpike. Follow Route 26 North to Norway, then turn left onto Route 117 and go 2 miles. Bear right onto Route 118. The course is less than a mile ahead on your left.
Course Description: The scorecard claims this to be "Maine's Most Scenic 9-Hole Golf Course," and the view from the first tee—about 50 feet above the fairway—backs up that claim. On a clear day, Mount Washington and area lakes and hills are visible in the distance. The course plays along the side of a hill covering former farmland. Fairways are relatively flat as a result, but most holes play either uphill or down, so the challenge is in judging wind and distance. The 415-yard par-4 fifth, for example, is all uphill and, according to locals, with any wind at all "is the longest 415 yards in the state." The par-3s at numbers two and six (180 and 167 yards, respectively) are the course's character holes. You don't want to stray right or left on these well-bunkered greens. The clubhouse—the former farmhouse—provides great views of lakes and mountains from its dining room and porch.
Courses Nearby: Paris Hill, Turner Highlands

OAKDALE GOLF CLUB

RIVER ROAD
MEXICO
207-364-3951
REGION: Western Lakes and Mountains
MAP: 19
ESTABLISHED: 1923
NUMBER OF HOLES: 9
COURSE LENGTH/PAR: Back: 6,198/72   **Front:** 5,755/74
COURSE RATING/SLOPE: Back: 68.8/119 **Front:** 73.6/125
HEAD PROFESSIONAL: Yes
COURSE ARCHITECT: NA
GOLF FACILITIES: Full pro shop, practice green, club rental, club repair, club storage, cart rental, pull-cart rental, instruction, locker room, showers, snack bar, lounge
TEE TIMES: Recommended
HOW LONG IN ADVANCE: 5 days
RANGER: Yes
TEE-OFF INTERVAL TIME: 10 minutes
TIME TO PLAY 18 HOLES: 4 hours, 15 minutes
EARLIEST TEE-OFF: 7 a.m.
GREEN FEES: Weekend (18): $$ Weekday (18): $
PAYMENT: MasterCard, Visa
SEASON: April 15 through October 31
LOCAL CHAMBER OF COMMERCE: River Valley, 207-364-3241
LOCAL ATTRACTIONS: Mount Blue State Park
DIRECTIONS: From Lewiston take Exit 12 off the Maine Turnpike. Follow Route 4 North to Route 108 in Livermore. Take Route 108 into Rumford. Turn right onto Route 2 (River Road) to Mexico. The course is 3 miles ahead on your left.
COURSE DESCRIPTION: This is the heart of paper- and timber-processing country. Built in 1923, the course plays into the Androscoggin River valley with fairways more rolling than hilly. A few holes are wide open, a few tree lined, and a couple will jump up and grab you. The 150-yard par-3 fourth features an elevated tee to an elevated green. The drop-off left or right is long and steep, and the green slopes back to front. It's a difficult target to hit—and a tough putt if you do. The fairway on the dogleg-left 340-yard seventh slopes left to right and kicks most tee shots into a small landing area, leaving a tough approach to a two-tiered green with a bunker at its back. Number eight is a mild-mannered 240-yard par-4 on the first loop but plays as a 200-yard par-3 as does number seventeen. Water just off the tee and a large bunker just in front of the small green make length and accuracy critical.
COURSES NEARBY: Bethel Inn, Maple Lane Inn, Wilson Lake

OLD ORCHARD BEACH COUNTRY CLUB

WILD DUNES WAY
OLD ORCHARD BEACH
207-934-4513
WEB: www.dunegrass.com
REGION: Southern Coast
MAP: 3
ESTABLISHED: 1920
NUMBER OF HOLES: 9
COURSE LENGTH/PAR: Back: 5,524/70   **Front:** 5,110/70
COURSE RATING/SLOPE: Back: 66.4/114 **Front:** 67.4/113
HEAD PROFESSIONAL: Yes
COURSE ARCHITECT: Alex Chisholm
GOLF FACILITIES: Full pro shop, driving range, practice green, practice bunker, club rental, club repair, club storage, cart rental, pull-cart rental, instruction, locker room, showers, restaurant, lounge
TEE TIMES: Not necessary
RANGER: Yes
TIME TO PLAY 18 HOLES: 4 hours
EARLIEST TEE-OFF: 6:30 a.m.
GREEN FEES: Weekend (18): $$ **Weekday (18): $**
PAYMENT: MasterCard, Visa, American Express
SEASON: April through November
LOCAL CHAMBER OF COMMERCE: Old Orchard Beach, 207-934-2500
LOCAL ATTRACTIONS: Old Orchard Beach, beaches
DIRECTIONS: From Exit 5 off the Maine Turnpike (I-95) take exit ramp 2A to Route 1 North. Travel 1/10 mile and take a right on Ross Road. Wild Dunes Way is 2 miles ahead on your right (part of the Dunegrass Golf Club complex).
COURSE DESCRIPTION: Adjacent to Dunegrass Golf Club and located in one of Maine's top tourist destinations, Old Orchard Beach Country Club has a rich and colorful past. Built in the 1920s, it was expanded to 18 holes in the 1930s. During its heyday, it earned a reputation as one of the top golf destinations in the Northeast, attracting golf exhibitions with some of the greatest golfers of the era, Gene Sarazen and Babe Didrickson Zaharias. As was the case with many 18-hole courses, World War II forced the closure and, in this case, sale of the second 9 and clubhouse. The course has operated as a nine-hole layout ever since. With the opening of Dunegrass Golf Club, Old Orchard became part of a 27-hole complex. Designed by Alex Chisholm, Maine's most renowned professional golfer, the course is fairly open and easily walkable, making it popular with beginners and seniors.
COURSES NEARBY: Biddeford-Saco, Cape Arundel, Dunegrass, Dutch Elm, Nonesuch River, Sable Oaks, Salmon Falls, Sanford, Willowdale

ORCHARD VIEW GOLF CLUB

GOLF COURSE ROAD
NEWPORT
207-368-5600
REGION: Kennebec/Moose River Region
MAP: 22
ESTABLISHED: Circa 1955
NUMBER OF HOLES: 9
COURSE LENGTH/PAR: Back: 4,480/60
COURSE RATING/SLOPE: Back: NA
HEAD PROFESSIONAL: No
COURSE ARCHITECT: NA
GOLF FACILITIES: Practice green, club rental, club repair, cart rental, pull-cart rental
TEE TIMES: Not necessary
RANGER: No
TIME TO PLAY 18 HOLES: 3 hours, 15 minutes
EARLIEST TEE-OFF: 7 a.m.
GREEN FEES: Weekend (18): $ Weekday (18): $
PAYMENT: Cash only
SEASON: Mid-April through September
LOCAL CHAMBER OF COMMERCE: Sebasticook Valley, 207-368-4698
LOCAL ATTRACTIONS: Sebasticook Lake, apples
DIRECTIONS: From Waterville take I-95 to Exit 39. Follow Route 7 North about 2 miles, then take a right onto Golf Course Road. The course is about 1/2 mile ahead on your left.
COURSE DESCRIPTION: This family-run course is ideal for beginners, but even more experienced golfers will find its long par-3s and small greens a suitable test. A few holes play amid an active apple orchard. Given the three par-4s—the longest and admittedly the toughest on the course being the 432-yard eighth—and four par-3s over 195 yards, you surely won't be leaving your woods at home. The course is well maintained, and current owners have invested a lot of time and energy into improving tee boxes, planting trees, and enlarging some greens. A former farm, the small clubhouse was once a potato barn.
COURSES NEARBY: Carmel Valley, J. W. Parks, Palmyra

PALMYRA GOLF COURSE

147 LANG HILL ROAD
PALMYRA
207-938-4947
WEB: www.palmyra-me.com
REGION: Kennebec/Moose River Region

MAP: 21

ESTABLISHED: 1987

NUMBER OF HOLES: 18

COURSE LENGTH/PAR: Back: 6,617/72 **Middle:** 6,367/72 **Front:** 5,464/72

COURSE RATING/SLOPE: Back: 70.1/120 **Middle:** 69.0/118 **Front:** 69.9/118

HEAD PROFESSIONAL: No

COURSE ARCHITECT: Brad Cayer

GOLF FACILITIES: Driving range, practice green, practice bunker, club rental, cart rental, pull-cart rental, instruction, snack bar, lounge

TEE TIMES: Recommended

HOW LONG IN ADVANCE: 1 week

RANGER: Yes

TEE-OFF INTERVAL TIME: 10 minutes

TIME TO PLAY 18 HOLES: 4 hours

EARLIEST TEE-OFF: 6:50 a.m.

GREEN FEES: Weekend (18): $ Weekday (18): $

PAYMENT: MasterCard, Visa

SEASON: April through October

LOCAL CHAMBER OF COMMERCE: Sebasticook Valley, 207-368-4698

LOCAL ATTRACTIONS: Sebasticook Lake, apples

DIRECTIONS: From Waterville take Exit 39 off I-95 (Newport). Head west on Route 2 for about 4 miles. Take a right onto Land Hill Road. The course is on your right.

COURSE DESCRIPTION: A family-owned and -operated golf course located between Waterville and Bangor. Formerly 9 holes, it expanded to 18 in the early 1990s with a completely new layout. The course features a little of everything, from open holes leading to small round greens to tight tree-lined fairways and tiered greens. The signature hole is without doubt the 575-yard par-5 third. Following two relatively easy opening par-4s, this broken dogleg left is straight-away for about 400 tree-lined yards before you can even see the green. Then there's a long uphill approach to a green guarded with sand. Pars are a rare treat on this hole. The 400-yard par-4 seventh is straightaway and tree lined but claims the best view of surrounding farms from its elevated tee. The back nine opens up a bit but has more water hazards. The 386-yard tenth, for example, has water on either side of its bean-shaped green. And while not open water, the tough 387-yard thirteenth leads with a blind tee shot, leaving an approach to the green made all the more difficult by trees and overgrowth that pinch the fairway from either side. The pond that makes up most of the 198-yard seventeenth reportedly gets more play than the practice range. The owners recently added a 50-site RV camp-ground complete with a camp store and recreational building, creating unique stay-and-play opportunities. Plans now are to remodel the clubhouse, expand the pro shop, and add other amenities.

COURSES NEARBY: Dexter Municipal, J. W. Parks, Orchard View

Paris Hill Country Club

Paris Hill Road
Paris
207-743-2371

Region: Western Lakes and Mountains
Map: 11
Established: 1899
Number of Holes: 9
Course Length/Par: Back: 4,637/66   **Front:** 4,118/66
Course Rating/Slope: Back: 62.1/102 **Front:** NA
Head Professional: Yes
Course Architect: Harvey Lamontagne (R)
Golf Facilities: Full pro shop, practice green, practice bunker, club rental, club storage, cart rental, pull-cart rental, instruction, snack bar, lounge
Tee Times: Not necessary
Ranger: No
Time to Play 18 Holes: 3 hours, 45 minutes
Earliest Tee-Off: 6:30 a.m.
Green Fees: Weekend (18): $ Weekday (18): $
Payment: Cash only
Season: April through October
Local Chamber of Commerce: Oxford Hills, 207-743-2281
Local Attractions: Hannibal Hamlin Museum, tourmaline mines, lakes, hiking
Directions: From Portland take Exit 11 off the Maine Turnpike. Follow Route 26 North to South Paris. Just outside town turn right onto Paris Hill Road. Follow to top of the hill. The course is on your right.
Course Description: Once the seat of Oxford County, picturesque Paris Hill is best known as the hometown of Hannibal Hamlin, Abraham Lincoln's vice president during his first term. A museum honoring Paris Hill's favorite son occupies the second floor of the town library, formerly a 19th-century jail just down the road from the course. Built in 1899, Paris Hill Country Club is, as its scorecard attests, "A Touch of the Past." Laid out on a nearly rectangular piece of property and virtually unchanged in its 100-year history, the course is a great example of golf at the turn of the century. Short and straightaway, holes are wide open with relatively few hazards other than the vintage man-made mounds guarding several of the greens. Greens are characteristically small and present tough targets. The stately 19th-century clubhouse does nothing to dispel the notion that you may have taken a step back in time.
Courses Nearby: Norway, Poland Spring, Turner Highlands

Penobscot Valley Country Club

366 Main Street
Orono
207-866-2423
Region: Katahdin/Moosehead Region
Map: 23
Established: 1924
Number of Holes: 18
Course Length/Par: Back: 6,445/72   **Middle:** 6,301/72   **Front:** 5,796/74
Course Rating/Slope: Back: 71.2/128 **Middle:** 70.5/126   **Front:** 73.9/128
Head Professional: Yes
Course Architect: Donald Ross
Golf Facilities: Full pro shop, driving range, practice green, practice bunker, club repair, club storage, cart rental, pull-cart rental, instruction, locker room, showers, restaurant, lounge
Tee Times: Necessary
How Long in Advance: 1 week
Ranger: Yes
Tee-Off Interval Time: 7 and 8 minutes
Time to Play 18 Holes: 4 hours, 15 minutes
Earliest Tee-Off: 7 a.m.; public not allowed till after 2 p.m. on weekends
Green Fees: Weekend (18): $$$$ **Weekday (18):** $$$$
Payment: MasterCard, Visa
Season: April 15 through October 30
Local Chamber of Commerce: Bangor Region, 207-947-0307
Local Attractions: University of Maine, Greater Bangor area
Directions: From Bangor take Exit 50 off I-95. Turn right onto Kelly Road and follow to its end. Turn right onto Route 2. The course is 500 yards ahead on your left.
Course Description: Just 15 minutes north of Bangor, Penobscot Valley was Maine's first full 18-hole golf course built from scratch. It also claims to be one of the few courses in the state that designer Donald Ross supervised on site during its construction. One of Maine's most highly regarded golf clubs, "Penobby" (as it is referred to by locals) has hosted several Maine Amateur Championships as well as attracting many name players including Tony Lema, Bob Toski, and Arnold Palmer. Despite its 75 years, many original design features—notably grass-faced bunkers and small, difficult greens—remain an integral part of the club's character. Although it's still fairly open, interestingly the biggest intentional change to the original layout has been the addition of trees, planted by members some 30 or 40 years ago. At 6,301 yards (from the white tees) and par 72, Penobscot Valley features some short par-5s but balances them with some tough par-4s. The 424-yard thirteenth, for example, presents a blind tee shot over a hill, leaving a long approach to a small, sloping green that drops off dramatically to the right. And

then there's the 425-yard eighteenth. Your drive needs to carry 225 yards to clear a gully and avoid a blind approach to a small, undulating green guarded by a bunker. The spacious clubhouse, a former farmhouse, is a great place to relax following your round. *Note: Public play is welcomed during the week but does not begin until after 2 p.m. on weekends.*

COURSES NEARBY: Bangor Municipal, Felt Brook, Hampden, Hermon Meadow, Hidden Meadows, Pine Hill

PINE HILL GOLF CLUB
OUTER MILL STREET
BREWER
207-989-3824
REGION: Katahdin/Moosehead Region
MAP: 23
ESTABLISHED: 1962
NUMBER OF HOLES: 9
COURSE LENGTH/PAR: Back: 5,799/71   **Front:** 5,100/72
COURSE RATING/SLOPE: Back: 63.0/92   **Front:** NA
HEAD PROFESSIONAL: No
COURSE ARCHITECT: Charles Emery
GOLF FACILITIES: Driving range, practice green, club rental, cart rental, pull-cart rental, instruction, snack bar
TEE TIMES: Not necessary
RANGER: Yes
TIME TO PLAY 18 HOLES: 4 hours
EARLIEST TEE-OFF: 7 a.m.
GREEN FEES: Weekend (18): $ Weekday (18): $
PAYMENT: Cash only
SEASON: April 20 through November 10
LOCAL CHAMBER OF COMMERCE: Bangor Region, 207-947-0307
LOCAL ATTRACTIONS: Greater Bangor, Bangor Mall
DIRECTIONS: From I-95 take Exit 45 to I-395. Take the South Main Street/Brewer Exit (Route 15 South). Turn left onto Outer Mill Street. Look for signs.
COURSE DESCRIPTION: Relatively flat, straight and wide open but with just enough trouble to make trouble. Prevailing winds cause a few holes, particularly the 498-yard sixth, to play longer than the card indicates. The small greens are well maintained and will hold an approach shot, so shooting at the flag is recommended. But if you are off line, you're just as likely to bounce and roll past the green through the closely cropped—make that nonexistent—rough. Small pro shop and friendly atmosphere.
COURSES NEARBY: Bangor Municipal, Felt Brook, Hampden, Hermon Meadows, Penobscot Valley

PINE HOLLOW LITTLE PAR 3
548 MAIN STREET
SANFORD
207-324-5271
REGION: Southern Coast
MAP: 2
ESTABLISHED: 1961
NUMBER OF HOLES: 18
COURSE LENGTH/PAR: Back: 931/54
COURSE RATING/SLOPE: Back: NA
HEAD PROFESSIONAL: Yes
COURSE ARCHITECT: Robert L'Heureux
GOLF FACILITIES: Practice green, club rental, instruction
TEE TIMES: Not necessary
RANGER: No
TIME TO PLAY 18 HOLES: 1 hour, 30 minutes
EARLIEST TEE-OFF: 9 a.m.
GREEN FEES: Weekend (18): $ Weekday (18): $
PAYMENT: Cash only
SEASON: April through September
LOCAL CHAMBER OF COMMERCE: Sanford/Springvale, 207-324-4280
LOCAL ATTRACTIONS: Area beaches
DIRECTIONS: From Exit 2 off the Maine Turnpike (I-95) follow Route 109 toward Sanford for 11 miles. The course is on your right.
COURSE DESCRIPTION: This short par-3 layout is great for beginners or to practice your short game. Holes range from 35 to 80 yards. Course record is a 44. Family owned and operated.
COURSES NEARBY: Sanford

PINE RIDGE MUNICIPAL GOLF COURSE
WEST RIVER ROAD
WATERVILLE
207-873-0474
REGION: Kennebec/Moose River Region
MAP: 21
ESTABLISHED: 1978
NUMBER OF HOLES: 9
COURSE LENGTH/PAR: Back: 2,570/54
COURSE RATING/SLOPE: Back: NA
HEAD PROFESSIONAL: No

COURSE ARCHITECT: NA

GOLF FACILITIES: Practice green, club rental, pull-cart rental

TEE TIMES: Not necessary

TIME TO PLAY 18 HOLES: 2 hours, 30 minutes

EARLIEST TEE-OFF: 7 a.m.

GREEN FEES: Weekend (18): $ Weekday (18): $

PAYMENT: Cash only

SEASON: April through September

LOCAL CHAMBER OF COMMERCE: Mid-Maine, 207-873-3315 or 3316

LOCAL ATTRACTIONS: Colby College

DIRECTIONS: From Exit 33 off I-95 head east on Route 11 (Kennedy Drive). After about 1 mile take a right onto Route 104 (West River Road). The course is less than a mile ahead.

COURSE DESCRIPTION: Owned by the city of Waterville, this par-3 course traverses hilly terrain. No water and few bunkers to contend with. Don't leave your woods at home, though—you'll need them on the 220-yard fifth. Ideal for beginning golfers.

COURSES NEARBY: Belgrade Lakes, Cedar Springs, Natanis, Waterville

PISCATAQUIS COUNTRY CLUB

DOVER ROAD

GUILFORD

207-876-3203

REGION: Katahdin/Moosehead Region

MAP: 31

ESTABLISHED: 1926

NUMBER OF HOLES: 9

COURSE LENGTH/PAR: Back: 5,414/69

COURSE RATING/SLOPE: Back: 64.6/112

HEAD PROFESSIONAL: Yes

COURSE ARCHITECT: NA

GOLF FACILITIES: Full pro shop, driving range, practice green, practice bunker, club rental, club repair, club storage, cart rental, pull-cart rental, instruction, locker room, showers, restaurant, lounge

TEE TIMES: Not necessary

RANGER: No

TIME TO PLAY 18 HOLES: 3 hours, 45 minutes

EARLIEST TEE-OFF: 7 a.m.

GREEN FEES: Weekend (18): $ Weekday (18): $

PAYMENT: Cash only

SEASON: Mid-April through mid-October

LOCAL CHAMBER OF COMMERCE: Southern Piscataquis County, 207-564-7533

LOCAL ATTRACTIONS: Sebec Lake

DIRECTIONS: Drive north on I-95 to Exit 39 (Newport). Follow Route 7 North to Dexter. Take Route 23 to Sangerville. Turn right onto Route 15 (Dover Road). The course is on your left.

COURSE DESCRIPTION: Trees and hills add challenge to this otherwise short, well-maintained northern Maine layout. The 251-yard par-4 third plays into a deep gully that leads steeply up to an elevated green. Woods on either side and bunkers to the left of the green make for an interesting blind approach. Accuracy helps at the 164-yard sixth, where it is all downhill to the small green that's ringed by trees with a ditch running along the front. There are no water hazards on the course, but most greens are guarded by bunkers.

COURSES NEARBY: Dexter Municipal, Foxcroft

PLEASANT HILL GOLF CLUB
38 CHAMBERLAIN ROAD
SCARBOROUGH
207-883-4425
REGION: Greater Portland Area
MAP: 3
ESTABLISHED: 1962
NUMBER OF HOLES: 9
COURSE LENGTH/PAR: Back: 4,786/68   **Front:** 4,786/68
COURSE RATING/SLOPE: Back: 62.3/87   **Front:** 62.3/87
HEAD PROFESSIONAL: Yes
COURSE ARCHITECT: Jim Jones and Lowell McLaughlin
GOLF FACILITIES: Practice green, club rental, pull-cart rental, instruction, snack bar
TEE TIMES: Not necessary
RANGER: No
TIME TO PLAY 18 HOLES: 3 hours, 30 minutes
EARLIEST TEE-OFF: 7 a.m.
GREEN FEES: Weekend (18): $ Weekday (18): $
PAYMENT: Cash only
SEASON: April through October
LOCAL CHAMBER OF COMMERCE: Greater Portland Region, 207-772-2811
LOCAL ATTRACTIONS: Maine Mall, Greater Portland area, Scarborough Downs, beaches
DIRECTIONS: Take Exit 6A off the Maine Turnpike to I-295, then the Route 1 South (Main St.) Exit to Scarborough. Turn left onto Pleasant Hill Road. After about 1 mile take another left onto Chamberlain Road.
COURSE DESCRIPTION: A short nine-hole track just south of the Maine Mall and

Portland. Fairly wide open with large greens and no par-5s, it is ideally suited for beginners. The longest hole on the course is the 366-yard seventh, which requires a tee shot over the only water on the course. The ninth, a 230-yard par-4, has pine trees that cut in front of the green from the left, adding drama to what might otherwise be a straightforward hole. Small golf shop, snack bar, and friendly atmosphere.

COURSES NEARBY: Biddeford-Saco, Gorham, Nonesuch River, Riverside Municipal, South Portland Municipal, Willowdale

POINT SEBAGO GOLF COURSE & RESORT
ROUTE 302
CASCO
207-655-2747
WEB: www.pointsebago.com
REGION: Western Lakes and Mountains
MAP: 5
ESTABLISHED: 1996
NUMBER OF HOLES: 18
COURSE LENGTH/PAR: Back: 7,002/72   **Middle:** 6,474/72   **Front:** 5,645/72
COURSE RATING/SLOPE: Back: 73.7/135   **Middle:** 71.3/130   **Front:** 67.5/122
HEAD PROFESSIONAL: Yes
COURSE ARCHITECT: Philip Wogan
GOLF FACILITIES: Full pro shop, driving range, practice green, practice bunker, club rental, cart rental, instruction, golf school, restaurant, lounge, accommodations
TEE TIMES: Recommended
HOW LONG IN ADVANCE: 7 days
RANGER: Yes
TEE-OFF INTERVAL TIME: 9 minutes
TIME TO PLAY 18 HOLES: 5 hours
EARLIEST TEE-OFF: 7 a.m.
GREEN FEES: Weekend (18): $$$$ **Weekday (18):** $$$$
PAYMENT: All major credit cards
SEASON: Late April through early November
LOCAL CHAMBER OF COMMERCE: Greater Windham, 207-892-8265
LOCAL ATTRACTIONS: Sebago Lake, swimming, boating
DIRECTIONS: From Portland take Exit 8 off the Maine Turnpike (I-95) to Route 302 North. Follow for 22 miles. The resort is on your left.
COURSE DESCRIPTION: This resort is located on the shores of Sebago Lake, Maine's second largest and most popular lake. Point Sebago was recognized by *Golf Digest* as one of the best new affordable courses in the country when it opened in 1996. The course plays to a healthy 6,474 yards from the white tees

but stretches to 7,002 from the tips. Accuracy is important, and there are several risk-reward opportunities for the big hitter. Point Sebago is well maintained and features large, undulating, and amply guarded greens. Holes are deceptively broad, because trees and rough often narrow sculpted fairways at strategic points. The 338-yard par-4 third plays from an elevated tee to a sloping green protected by bunkers front and right, and by grassy knolls behind. Water cuts across the fairway about 130 yards out, and the remaining approach gets progressively narrower. The ninth is a classic dogleg right. It is every bit of 418 yards to an elevated green with bunkers left and right. The signature hole is the 302-yard fifteenth. It's a sharp dogleg left; a pond that runs up the left side to the green and bunkers along the right should dispel any notions of taking advantage of this tantalizingly short par-4. Stay-and-play packages are available. The resort has beach and restaurant facilities.

COURSES NEARBY: Bridgton Highlands, Fairlawn, Frye Island, Naples, Poland Spring, Spring Meadows, Summit

POLAND SPRING COUNTRY CLUB
ROUTE 26, 41 RICKER ROAD
POLAND SPRING
207-998-6002
WEB: www.polandspringinns.com
REGION: Western Lakes and Mountains
MAP: 5
ESTABLISHED: 1893
NUMBER OF HOLES: 18
COURSE LENGTH/PAR: Back: 5,830/71   **Front:** 5,603/71
COURSE RATING/SLOPE: Back: 68.2/119 **Front:** 71.6/119
HEAD PROFESSIONAL: No
COURSE ARCHITECT: Arthur H. Fenn (O9), Donald Ross (R, A9)
GOLF FACILITIES: Full pro shop, practice green, club rental, cart rental, pull-cart rental, locker room, restaurant, lounge, accommodations
TEE TIMES: Necessary
HOW LONG IN ADVANCE: One year
RANGER: Yes
TEE-OFF INTERVAL TIME: 8 minutes
TIME TO PLAY 18 HOLES: 4 hours, 15 minutes
EARLIEST TEE-OFF: Sunrise
GREEN FEES: Weekend (18): $$ Weekday (18): $$
PAYMENT: MasterCard, Visa, American Express
SEASON: May 1 through November 1
LOCAL CHAMBER OF COMMERCE: Androscoggin County, 207-783-2249
LOCAL ATTRACTIONS: Poland Spring, Maine State Building, Range Ponds State Park

DIRECTIONS: Take Exit 11 off the Maine Turnpike to Route 26 North. The course (at the inns at Poland Spring) is about 10 miles ahead on your right.

COURSE DESCRIPTION: Reputed to be the oldest continually operated resort course in America, Poland Spring's original nine was designed by Arthur H. Fenn, who at the time (1896) was an accomplished golfer and course architect. Built on the grounds of the 300-room Poland Spring House, a turn-of-the-century spa noted for the medicinal effects of its nearby springwaters, the original course was remodeled and a new nine added by Donald Ross in 1913. It played host to the Maine State Golf Association's first Maine Open, won appropriately by none other than Arthur Fenn himself. Although the hotel no longer exists, the original layout remains virtually intact today. Scenic and hilly are the terms that best describe Poland Spring's 5,830-yard track. The 412-yard par-4 fourth is a case in point. All downhill, you'll need to negotiate its narrow tree-lined fairway all the way to the green. The view of nearby Lower Range Pond, however, is a worthy distraction. For the most part, the course is open and its sloping greens are what make it a good test. Typical of its vintage, there is opportunity for bump-and-run shots but plenty of sand to catch the errant approach. The former ski lodge for the original resort serves as the clubhouse.

COURSES NEARBY: Apple Valley, Fairlawn, Norway, Paris Hill, Point Sebago, Prospect Hill, Spring Meadows, Summit

PORTAGE HILLS COUNTRY CLUB
ROUTE 11 NORTH
PORTAGE
207-435-8221
REGION: Aroostook
MAP: 64
ESTABLISHED: 1971
NUMBER OF HOLES: 9

COURSE LENGTH/PAR: Back: 6,164/72   **Front:** 5,718/74
COURSE RATING/SLOPE: Back: 69.5/110 **Front:** NA
HEAD PROFESSIONAL: No
COURSE ARCHITECT: Ben Gray
GOLF FACILITIES: Driving range, practice green, practice bunker, club rental, cart rental, pull-cart rental, snack bar, lounge
TEE TIMES: Not necessary
RANGER: No
TIME TO PLAY 18 HOLES: 4 hours
EARLIEST TEE-OFF: 7 a.m.
GREEN FEES: Weekend (18): $ Weekday (18): $
PAYMENT: Cash only
SEASON: April through September
LOCAL CHAMBER OF COMMERCE: Presque Isle Area, 207-764-6561

LOCAL ATTRACTIONS: Portage Lake, hunting, fishing

DIRECTIONS: Take I-95 to Houlton, then follow Route 1 North to Presque Isle. Turn left onto Route 163 to Ashland, then right onto Route 11 North to Portage. The course is just north of town.

COURSE DESCRIPTION: One of Maine's more remote golfing locales, Portage Hills was laid out by Canadian Ben Gray, designer of several other Aroostook County courses. As its name implies, the course is hilly, and it's not often easy to find a level lie. Greens, too, are small and sloping. A good deal of its play comes from summer visitors who vacation in camps surrounding Portage Lake. Very informal and friendly atmosphere.

COURSES NEARBY: Presque Isle Country Club

PRESQUE ISLE COUNTRY CLUB
ROUTE 205, PARKHURST SIDING ROAD
PRESQUE ISLE
207-764-0430

REGION: Aroostook

MAP: 65

ESTABLISHED: 1958

NUMBER OF HOLES: 18

COURSE LENGTH/PAR: Back: 6,730/72   **Middle:** 6,326/72   **Front:** 5,600/72

COURSE RATING/SLOPE: Back: 71.4/122   **Middle:** 69.1/117   **Front:** 72.5/119

HEAD PROFESSIONAL: Yes

COURSE ARCHITECT: Ben Gray (O9); Rick Hobbs & Geoffrey Cornish (A9–1987)

GOLF FACILITIES: Full pro shop, driving range, practice green, practice bunker, club rental, club repair, club storage, cart rental, pull-cart rental, instruction, locker room, showers, restaurant, lounge

TEE TIMES: Not necessary

RANGER: Yes

TEE-OFF INTERVAL TIME: 8 minutes

TIME TO PLAY 18 HOLES: 4 hours, 20 minutes

EARLIEST TEE-OFF: 7 a.m.

GREEN FEES: Weekend (18): $$ **Weekday (18): $$**

PAYMENT: MasterCard, Visa

SEASON: May 1 through November 1

LOCAL CHAMBER OF COMMERCE: Presque Isle Area, 207-764-6561

LOCAL ATTRACTIONS: Potato festivals, Fort Fairfield block house, hiking, University of Maine Presque Isle

DIRECTIONS: From Bangor take I-95 North to Houlton, then Route 1 North to Presque Isle. Turn right onto Route 167. After about 3 miles turn left onto Route 205 (Parkhurst Siding Road). The course is on your right.

COURSE DESCRIPTION: The town of Presque Isle is Aroostook County's largest and fastest-growing community. The original nine at Presque Isle Country Club was designed by Canadian architect Ben Gray in 1958. In 1984 the club pro, Rick Hobbs, and architect Geoffrey Cornish collaborated on a new nine that is incorporated into the original layout. Stretching 6,730 yards (from the back tees) over former potato fields, the 18-hole track traverses a rolling landscape providing picturesque views of the Aroostook River and neighboring hills. Appropriately, Presque Isle plays host to the annual Spudland Open, which draws golfers from all over the Northeast and Canada. Many locals say if you survive the first five holes here, you'll score well. The formidable 423-yard par-4 fifth is perhaps most responsible for this claim. The narrow tree-lined approach off this undulating fairway is blind, and the green is guarded by bunkers left and right. Accuracy is critical. Requiring equal adeptness is the seemingly tame 103-yard sixteenth. Your blind tee shot needs to land on a tree-encircled green that drops off significantly on all sides. A large, comfortable clubhouse complements an enjoyable golf experience.

COURSES NEARBY: Aroostook Valley, Caribou, Limestone, Mars Hill, Portage

PROSPECT HILL GOLF COURSE

694 SOUTH MAIN STREET
AUBURN
207-782-9220
REGION: Western Lakes and Mountains
MAP: 5
ESTABLISHED: 1957
NUMBER OF HOLES: 18
COURSE LENGTH/PAR: Back: 5,846/71   **Front:** 5,227/73
COURSE RATING/SLOPE: Back: 67.6/114 **Front:** 69.7/116
HEAD PROFESSIONAL: Yes
COURSE ARCHITECT: Arthur David Chapman
GOLF FACILITIES: Full pro shop, practice green, club rental, club repair, club storage, cart rental, pull-cart rental, instruction, locker room, snack bar, lounge
TEE TIMES: Not necessary
RANGER: Yes
TIME TO PLAY 18 HOLES: 4 hours, 15 minutes
EARLIEST TEE-OFF: 6 a.m.
GREEN FEES: Weekend (18): $ Weekday (18): $
PAYMENT: MasterCard, Visa, Discover
SEASON: April 15 through November 15
LOCAL CHAMBER OF COMMERCE: Androscoggin County, 207-783-2249
LOCAL ATTRACTIONS: Bradbury Mountain State Park
DIRECTIONS: From Exit 12 off the Maine Turnpike (I-495) follow Route 202 into Auburn. Take a right onto South Main (Route 136). Follow signs to golf course.

COURSE DESCRIPTION: The front nine at Prospect Hill was built in 1957, and the back nine was added in 1968. Although designed by the same person, the sides have two distinct personalities. The opening holes cover land once used as a dairy farm and are characteristically open, with few trees, a couple of small ponds, and greens on the small side. In contrast, the back side is more tree lined, has five ponds that come into play, and features large greens. In other words, build up your ego on the front, because it may be tempered coming in. The 366-yard sixteenth, for example, features a large pond that crosses the fairway where most mortals would be landing a drive. (It takes about 240 yards to clear it.) The only option is to lay up, thereby turning a relatively modest par-4 into quite a long one. Many of the tees have been enlarged, and six forward tees have been added. Several new bunkers are planned, and a vigorous tree-planting program is in place.

COURSES NEARBY: Apple Valley, Fairlawn, Poland Spring, Springbrook, Summit, Turner Highlands

RIVERMEADOW GOLF CLUB
216 LINCOLN STREET
WESTBROOK
207-854-1625
REGION: Greater Portland Area
MAP: 5
ESTABLISHED: 1958
NUMBER OF HOLES: 9
COURSE LENGTH/PAR: Back: 5,674/70   **Front:** 5,328/72
COURSE RATING/SLOPE: Back: 66.9/117 **Front:** 69.4/117
HEAD PROFESSIONAL: Yes
COURSE ARCHITECT: Rufus Jordan, Dick Dennison
GOLF FACILITIES: Full pro shop, practice green, club rental, club repair, cart rental, pull-cart rental, instruction, snack bar, lounge
TEE TIMES: Not necessary
RANGER: Yes
TIME TO PLAY 18 HOLES: 4 hours, 15 minutes
EARLIEST TEE-OFF: 7 a.m.
GREEN FEES: Weekend (18): $ Weekday (18): $
PAYMENT: Cash only
SEASON: April 1 through November 15
LOCAL CHAMBER OF COMMERCE: Greater Portland Region, 207-772-2811
LOCAL ATTRACTIONS: Maine Mall, Greater Portland area
DIRECTIONS: From Exit 8 off the Maine Turnpike (I-95) follow Business Route 25 into Westbrook. Turn right onto Bridge Street, then take the first left on Lincoln Street to the club.
COURSE DESCRIPTION: One of several Greater Portland–area courses,

Rivermeadow features broad, flat fairways that, in many cases, are divided by tall stands of white pine trees. The second hole is certainly the most memorable and will test the best shot maker's skill. A 411-yard dogleg right, this par-4 requires a drive of about 200 yards to get to the corner. The small green sits to the left, so even a good drive means you have to draw the ball into the green. It certainly earns its number one handicap ranking. A pond comes into play on the 455-yard par-5 ninth, which also has out of bounds along the right and thick trees along the left. The club's parking area is just beyond the green. You might want to keep this in mind when you're looking for a place to park.

COURSES NEARBY: Gorham, Sable Oaks, Twin Falls, Val Halla

RIVERSIDE MUNICIPAL GOLF COURSE
1158 RIVERSIDE STREET
PORTLAND
207-797-3524 OR 5588
REGION: Greater Portland Area
MAP: 3
ESTABLISHED: 1932
NUMBER OF HOLES: 27
COURSE LENGTH/PAR (NORTH COURSE): Back: 6,353/72 **Middle:** 5,947/72 **Front:** 5,332/72
COURSE RATING/SLOPE (NORTH COURSE): Back: 69.2/115 **Middle:** 67.5/NA **Front:** 70.1/112
HEAD PROFESSIONAL: Yes
COURSE ARCHITECT: Wayne Stiles, William F. Mitchell (R), Cornish & Silva (A9)
GOLF FACILITIES: Full pro shop, driving range, practice green, club rental, club repair, club storage, cart rental, pull-cart rental, instruction, locker room, showers, restaurant, lounge
TEE TIMES: Necessary on weekends and holidays only
HOW LONG IN ADVANCE: 3 days
RANGER: Yes
TEE-OFF INTERVAL TIME: 7 minutes
TIME TO PLAY 18 HOLES: 4 hours
EARLIEST TEE-OFF: 7 a.m.
GREEN FEES: Weekend (18): $$　　　　**Weekday (18): $**
PAYMENT: MasterCard, Visa
SEASON: April through November 15
LOCAL CHAMBER OF COMMERCE: Greater Portland Region, 207-772-2811
LOCAL ATTRACTIONS: Greater Portland, Maine Mall, Casco Bay islands
DIRECTIONS: Take Exit 8 off the Maine Turnpike (I-95) and turn right onto Riverside Street. Drive straight through three sets of lights. The course is about 2 miles ahead on your left.

COURSE DESCRIPTION: Located in Maine's largest city, Riverside's 27-hole complex—the 18-hole North Course and the 9-hole South Course—is a highly regarded municipal facility. In 1967 the city commissioned Geoffrey Cornish to lay out an additional nine holes to help accommodate the volume of play. Until recently the older 18-hole North Course was a regular host to the Maine Open. Its front nine is tree lined but with broad fairways. The back side, a few holes of which border the Presumpscot River, is narrower and little less forgiving. The terrain is hilly but easily walkable. Greens are well maintained considering the amount of traffic they receive. The par-3s here can be tough, particularly the 185-yard third that plays downhill to a small, well-guarded green. The 414-yard par-4 twelfth is a dogleg right that requires a good tee shot to make the corner—and still leaves a long approach.

COURSES NEARBY: Gorham, Nonesuch River, Pleasant Hill, Sable Oaks, South Portland, Twin Falls, Val Halla, Willowdale

ROCKLAND GOLF CLUB
606 OLD COUNTY ROAD
ROCKLAND
207-594-9322
REGION: Mid-Coast Region
MAP: 14
ESTABLISHED: 1932
NUMBER OF HOLES: 18
COURSE LENGTH/PAR: Back: 6,121/70   **Middle:** 5,491/70   **Front:** 5,583/73
COURSE RATING/SLOPE: Back: 69.2/118 **Middle:** 67.8/115 **Front:** 71.8/119
HEAD PROFESSIONAL: Yes
COURSE ARCHITECT: Wayne Stiles (O9), Roger Sorrent (A9)
GOLF FACILITIES: Full pro shop, practice green, practice bunker, club rental, club repair, club storage, cart rental, pull-cart rental, instruction, locker room, showers, restaurant, lounge
TEE TIMES: Necessary
HOW LONG IN ADVANCE: 2 days
RANGER: Yes
TEE-OFF INTERVAL TIME: 8 minutes
TIME TO PLAY 18 HOLES: 4 hours
EARLIEST TEE-OFF: 7 a.m.
GREEN FEES: Weekend (18): $$$ **Weekday (18): $$$**
PAYMENT: MasterCard, Visa
SEASON: April 1 through October 31
LOCAL CHAMBER OF COMMERCE: Rockland-Thomaston Area, 207-596-0376
LOCAL ATTRACTIONS: Lobster Festival, Farnsworth Museum, Owls Head Transportation Museum, windjammers

DIRECTIONS: From Portland take Exit 22 off I-95 in Brunswick. Follow Route 1 to Rockland, turning left onto Route 17 West. After about 1 mile turn right at the light onto Old County Road. The course is 1/2 mile ahead on your left.

COURSE DESCRIPTION: This 5,941-yard par-70 design was originally laid out as a nine-hole affair by Wayne Stiles in 1932. The course's builder and longtime greenskeeper Roger Sorrent was engaged to modify and add a new nine in 1965. The result is a fairly wide-open course with just enough challenges to reward all levels of play. The short 266-yard par-4 third, for example, is easily reachable in regulation, but the slick two-tiered green presents ample opportunity to three-putt. Some long par-3s at nine and eleven (216 and 219 yards, respectively) lead up to the number one handicap hole: the 440-yard par-4 thirteenth. A blind tee shot on this dogleg left leaves you with a long downhill approach to a small green with bunkers on either side. The tee at fifteen boasts a splendid view of nearby Lake Chickawaukie and the green—585 yards distant. The par-3 eighteenth requires a tee shot over water—one of several former lime quarries in the area—to a well-protected green. The modern clubhouse has a restaurant serving breakfast and lunch, a comfortable lounge area, and wraparound porch with commanding views of the lake and surrounding hills.

COURSES NEARBY: Goose River, North Haven, Samoset Resort

SABLE OAKS GOLF CLUB

505 COUNTRY CLUB DRIVE
SOUTH PORTLAND
207-775-6257

REGION: Greater Portland Area

MAP: 3

ESTABLISHED: 1989

NUMBER OF HOLES: 18

COURSE LENGTH/PAR: Back: 6,359/70   **Middle:** 6,056/70   **Front:** 4,786/72

COURSE RATING/SLOPE: Back: 71.0/138 **Middle:** 70.4/134   **Front:** 69.4/116

HEAD PROFESSIONAL: Yes

COURSE ARCHITECT: Cornish & Silva

GOLF FACILITIES: Full pro shop, practice green, club rental, cart rental, pull-cart rental, instruction, locker room, showers, restaurant, lounge

TEE TIMES: Recommended

HOW LONG IN ADVANCE: 7 days

RANGER: Yes

TEE-OFF INTERVAL TIME: 8 minutes

TIME TO PLAY 18 HOLES: 4 hours, 30 minutes

EARLIEST TEE-OFF: 6 a.m.

GREEN FEES: Weekend (18): $$$ **Weekday (18): $$**

PAYMENT: MasterCard, Visa, Discover

Season: April 1 till snowfall

Local Chamber of Commerce: Greater Portland Region, 207-772-2811

Local Attractions: Maine Mall, Greater Portland area, Portland Sea Dogs

Directions: From Exit 7 off the Maine Turnpike (I-95) follow Maine Mall Road north past the mall to Running Hill Road. Turn left, then take the second right onto Country Club Drive.

Course Description: Since it opened 10 years ago, Sable Oaks has always ranked as one of the state's top golf courses. Designed by Geoffrey Cornish and Brian Silva, the current 6,056-yard par-70 track (6,359 yards from the tips) plays to a tough 134 slope. Fairways are narrow; greens are big, fast, and sloping; and bunkers are plentiful. Most holes leave little margin for error. Under new ownership in 1999, management has vowed to "soften" the course, making it more playable for the high handicapper while maintaining the challenge for the good golfer. Changes in store include new tee boxes, tree cutting and brush clearing, and converting a few sand bunkers to grass. At 443 yards, the signature par-5 fourteenth is a classic risk-and-reward hole. Jackson Brook cuts across the narrow fairway about 230 yards out from the tee and then winds its way immediately in front of the green. Somewhat hilly with lots of ledge outcroppings and towering trees, it's a peaceful setting. It's sometimes hard to believe this course sits minutes away from the Maine Mall and Portland Jetport. A modern shingle-style clubhouse with a new restaurant complements a great golf experience.

Courses Nearby: Dunegrass, Gorham, Nonesuch River, Old Orchard, Riverside Municipal, Rivermeadow, South Portland, Val Halla, Westerly Winds, Willowdale

St. Croix Country Club
River Road
Calais
207-454-8875

Region: Acadia/Down East

Map: 36

Established: 1930

Number of Holes: 9

Course Length/Par: Back: 5,470/68   **Front:** 5,370/72

Course Rating/Slope: Back: 64.8/102 **Front:** 68.5/111

Head Professional: Yes

Course Architect: NA

Golf Facilities: Full pro shop, club rental, club repair, club storage, cart rental, pull-cart rental, instruction, showers, snack bar, lounge

Tee Times: Not necessary

Ranger: Yes

Time to Play 18 Holes: 4 hours

Earliest Tee-Off: 7 a.m.

Green Fees: Weekend (18): $$ **Weekday (18): $$**

PAYMENT: MasterCard, Visa

SEASON: Late April through November 1

LOCAL CHAMBER OF COMMERCE: Calais Region, 207-454-2308

LOCAL ATTRACTIONS: St. Croix Island Historical Site, Moosehorn Wildlife Refuge, Canadian border

DIRECTIONS: Follow Route 1 East from the Calais business district. The course is 1 mile ahead.

COURSE DESCRIPTION: The easternmost golf course in the United States, St. Croix has a signature seventh hole that was featured in the USGA's Golf Journal for its distinction as the first U.S. golf hole to receive sunlight in the new millennium. A 300-yard severe dogleg right, the seventh's green is framed by trees where an eagle's nest has been regularly occupied for the past several years. A layout more open than tight, the course features a nice variety of holes with small and sometimes tricky greens. Views of the St. Croix River highlight this scenic layout.

COURSES NEARBY: Great Cove

SALMON FALLS COUNTRY CLUB

SALMON FALLS ROAD

HOLLIS

207-929-5233

WEB: www.salmonfallsresort.com

REGION: Southern Coast

MAP: 2

ESTABLISHED: 1962

NUMBER OF HOLES: 9

COURSE LENGTH/PAR: Back: 5,848/72   **Front:** 5,193/70

COURSE RATING/SLOPE: Back: 67.6/121 **Front:** 69.5/112

HEAD PROFESSIONAL: Yes

COURSE ARCHITECT: Jim Jones

GOLF FACILITIES: Full pro shop, practice green, club rental, club repair, cart rental, pull-cart rental, instruction, restaurant, snack bar, lounge, accommodations

TEE TIMES: Recommended

HOW LONG IN ADVANCE: 1 week

RANGER: Yes

TEE-OFF INTERVAL TIME: 8 minutes

TIME TO PLAY 18 HOLES: 4 hours, 30 minutes

EARLIEST TEE-OFF: 6:30 a.m.

GREEN FEES: Weekend (18): $$ **Weekday (18): $$**

PAYMENT: All major credit cards

SEASON: April through October

LOCAL CHAMBER OF COMMERCE: Biddeford-Saco, 207-282-1567

LOCAL ATTRACTIONS: Historic area

DIRECTIONS: Take Exit 5 (Industrial Park Road) off the Maine Turnpike (I-95). Take a left onto Industrial Park Road and drive to the light, then turn right onto Route 112. After 6 miles take a left onto Route 117. The first right over the river is Salmon Falls Road. The course is on your right.

COURSE DESCRIPTION: Rather than calling themselves a "country club," the owners of Salmon Falls refer to this picturesque track as "a club in the country." Equidistant between Saco and Gorham, the nine-hole layout plays in full view of the Saco River. In fact, the river comes into play on the 365-yard first hole, where a left-to-right-sloping fairway will funnel errant shots to the water's edge. Two sets of tees give the front and back different looks. The 190-yard par-3 third stretches to 235 yards, as does the twelfth. A large pond makes the latter the number one handicap hole. The uphill 404-yard dogleg-left ninth is a great finishing hole. Along the right side of the ninth fairway is an eight-room motel that is part of the property. The clubhouse has a restaurant and snack bar facilities.

COURSES NEARBY: Dunegrass, Gorham, Nonesuch River, Willowdale

SAMOSET RESORT GOLF CLUB
220 WARRENTON STREET
ROCKPORT
207-594-2511

WEB: www.samoset.com

REGION: Mid-Coast Region

MAP: 14

ESTABLISHED: 1984

NUMBER OF HOLES: 18

COURSE LENGTH/PAR: Back: 6,548/70   **Middle:** 6,018/70   **Front:** 5,087/72

COURSE RATING/SLOPE: Back: 70.8/129 **Middle:** 69.7/125   **Front:** 70.1/120

HEAD PROFESSIONAL: Yes

COURSE ARCHITECT: Bob Elder

GOLF FACILITIES: Full pro shop, driving range, practice green, practice bunker, club rental, club storage, cart rental, pull-cart rental, instruction, golf school, locker room, showers, restaurant, lounge, accommodations

TEE TIMES: Necessary

HOW LONG IN ADVANCE: 2 days

RANGER: Yes

TEE-OFF INTERVAL TIME: 8 minutes

TIME TO PLAY 18 HOLES: 4 hours, 30 minutes

EARLIEST TEE-OFF: 7 a.m.

GREEN FEES: Weekend (18): $$$$ Weekday (18): $$$$

PAYMENT: All major credit cards

SEASON: Mid-April through mid-November

LOCAL CHAMBER OF COMMERCE: Camden-Rockport-Lincolnville, 207-236-4404

LOCAL ATTRACTIONS: Windjammers, Farnsworth Art Museum, Lobster Festival

DIRECTIONS: From Brunswick take Route 1 North through Rockland. Turn right onto Warrenton Avenue. The course is 1/2 mile ahead on your right.

COURSE DESCRIPTION: One of the most celebrated courses in the state, the Samoset perennially ranks near the top of *Golf Digest*'s Most Beautiful and Best Resort Course lists. It's been dubbed the "Pebble Beach of the East," and for good reason. Fourteen holes either border on or have a view of Penobscot Bay and the surrounding islands. Designed by Bob Elder in the late 1970s, the current layout was remodeled by Geoffrey Cornish in the 1980s and most recently by Ogunquit-based Brad Booth. To accommodate a planned 200-room facility, Booth was brought in to remodel the signature fourth hole (arguably one of the prettiest in the state) and convert number five from an unassuming par-4 to near perfect par-3. The picturesque fourth still plays as a dogleg left following the contours of the ocean shoreline. The revamped and heavily-bunkered green now backs up to a newly built seawall and the mile-long Rockland Breakwater beyond. It's a make-able par hole if you can concentrate on golf and not the view. The 180-yard fifth plays slightly uphill to a large diagonally oriented green guarded front right by a formidable cluster of bunkers. Numbers eleven, twelve, and thirteen offer an interesting par 3–5–3 sequence that includes water, trees, and more water. All of which lead up to the 435-yard dogleg-left par-4 sixteenth, with its long, narrow green and deserving of its number one handicap ranking. The Samoset recently built a new clubhouse with a large restaurant/lounge, full pro shop, and video golf facility. The 150-room resort's facilities include an indoor and outdoor pool and health club. In 1999 the resort came under new ownership, and many changes are in the works.

COURSES NEARBY: Goose River, North Haven, Rockland

SANDY RIVER GOLF COURSE

GEORGE THOMAS ROAD
FARMINGTON FALLS
207-778-2492

REGION: Western Lakes and Mountains

MAP: 20

ESTABLISHED: 1968

NUMBER OF HOLES: 9

COURSE LENGTH/PAR: Back: 3,612/64

COURSE RATING/SLOPE: Back: NA/NA

HEAD PROFESSIONAL: No

COURSE ARCHITECT: NA

GOLF FACILITIES: Driving range, practice green, practice bunker, club rental, pull-cart rental, snack bar

TEE TIMES: Not necessary

Ranger: No
Time to Play 18 Holes: 2 hours, 30 minutes
Earliest Tee-Off: 6:30 a.m.
Green Fees: Weekend (18): $ Weekday (18): $
Payment: Cash only
Season: Mid-April through November 15
Local Chamber of Commerce: Greater Farmington, 207-778-4215
Local Attractions: University of Maine, Farmington, Farmington Fair
Directions: From Exit 31 off I-95 follow Route 27 North to Route 2 in New Sharon. Turn left onto Route 2, and in about 5 miles take another left onto Route 41. George Thomas Road is on your left.
Course Description: A former par-3 course expanded in 1999, Sandy River features a fairly flat layout with small greens. Ideal for beginners. The 258-yard par-4 sixth (one of three par-4s on the course) will require an approach over a ravine, which you'll need to negotiate again on your blind tee shot at the 143-yard seventh. The longest hole on the course is the 308-yard ninth. The pro shop at Sandy River is, understandably, a small one offering few amenities.
Courses Nearby: Belgrade Lakes, Wilson Lake

Sanford Country Club
Route 4
Sanford
207-324-5462
Region: Southern Coast
Map: 2
Established: 1927
Number of Holes: 18
Course Length/Par: Back: 6,726/72   **Middle:** 6,217/72   **Front:** 5,320/74
Course Rating/Slope: Back: 73.2/128 **Middle:** 70.5/122 **Front:** 71.1/121
Head Professional: Yes
Course Architect: Alex Chisholm (O9), Marvin Armstrong (A9—1997)
Golf Facilities: Full pro shop, driving range, practice green, club rental, club repair, cart rental, pull-cart rental, instruction, locker room, snack bar, lounge
Tee Times: Necessary
How Long in Advance: Two days
Ranger: Yes
Time to Play 18 Holes: 4 hours, 30 minutes
Earliest Tee-Off: 6:30 a.m.
Green Fees: Weekend (18): $$$ Weekday (18): $$$
Payment: MasterCard, Visa
Season: April through October

LOCAL CHAMBER OF COMMERCE: Sanford/Springvale, 207-324-4280

LOCAL ATTRACTIONS: Area beaches

DIRECTIONS: From the Maine Turnpike (I-95) take Exit 2. Turn right onto Route 9, follow this into Sanford, and turn left onto Route 4. The course is about 3 miles ahead on your left.

COURSE DESCRIPTION: In 1997 Marvin Armstrong seamlessly integrated nine new holes into one of Maine pro/designer Alex Chisholm's best designs. Except for obvious signs of maturity, it's hard to tell the original holes from the new ones. It's a testament to the club owners' insistence upon commitment to maintaining the charm of this classic layout, which over its history has attracted the likes of Sam Snead, Jimmy Demaret, and Lanny Wadkins. The front nine throws everything at you, from the 100-yard par-3 fourth requiring a tee shot over water to a large tiered green, to the 488-yard par-5 third that doglegs just enough to thwart most attempts to get on—or even close—in two. The back side presents two successive par-5s at the 440-yard thirteenth and 488-yard fourteenth. The latter is a double dogleg that is narrow and slightly uphill, earning it a reputation as one of the toughest holes on the course. The 384-yard fifteenth has a memorable steeply uphill approach that, if left short, could end up right back at your feet. Water snakes around three sides of the landing area (thick rough makes up what's left) on the short par-4 sixteenth. The picturesque red shingle-style clubhouse adds to the club's friendly atmosphere and charm.

COURSES NEARBY: Biddeford-Saco, Cape Arundel, Dutch Elm, Highland Links, The Ledges, Links at Outlook, West Newfield

SEARSPORT PINES GOLF COURSE

240 MOUNT EPHRAIM ROAD

SEARSPORT

207-548-2854

REGION: Mid-Coast Region

MAP: 14

ESTABLISHED: 1999

NUMBER OF HOLES: 9

COURSE LENGTH/PAR: Back: 5,766/70   **Middle:** 5,360/70   **Front:** 4,732/72

COURSE RATING/SLOPE: Back: 65.4/107 **Middle:** 71.4/121   **Front:** 70.2/118

HEAD PROFESSIONAL: No

COURSE ARCHITECT: Bert Whitten

GOLF FACILITIES: Club rental, cart rental, pull-cart rental, snack bar

TEE TIMES: Necessary on weekends and holidays only

HOW LONG IN ADVANCE: 1 day

RANGER: Yes

TEE-OFF INTERVAL TIME: 8 minutes

TIME TO PLAY 18 HOLES: 3 hours

EARLIEST TEE-OFF: 7 a.m.

GREEN FEES: Weekend (18): $ Weekday (18): $

PAYMENT: MasterCard, Visa

SEASON: April through October 31

LOCAL CHAMBER OF COMMERCE: Belfast Area, 207-338-5900

LOCAL ATTRACTIONS: Penobscot Marine Museum, B&Bs

DIRECTIONS: From Belfast follow Route 1 North to Searsport. Turn left onto Mount Ephraim Road. The course is 2 miles ahead on your left.

COURSE DESCRIPTION: Perhaps better known as the home of sea captains and four-masted schooners, one of Maine's newest nine-hole courses opened in the coastal village of Searsport. This course was designed by owner Bert Whitten who, following his retirement as a university professor, returned to Maine and decided to convert the family farm into a golf course. The result of nearly three years of effort is this gem of a nine-hole layout. Just 5,766 yards from the back tees (18 holes), the course offers several risk reward opportunities and plenty of challenge for all golfers. The 490-yard dogleg-left par-5 eighth is the toughest on the course. A good drive leaves about 220 yards—all uphill—to a small green. The picturesque fairway is lined with 100-year-old pine trees all 80 to 90 feet high. The ninth is a great finisher. With a tee that runs around a pond reaching right up to the green, this par-3 can be anywhere from 105 to 135 yards. Bail out long and you're faced with a delicate chip back to an undulating putting surface that slopes toward the water. A converted country store serves as the pro shop.

COURSES NEARBY: Bucksport, Country View, Northport, Streamside

SHORE ACRES GOLF CLUB

SEBASCO HARBOR RESORT
SEBASCO ESTATES
207-389-9060

WEB: www.sebasco.com

REGION: Mid-Coast Region

MAP: 6

ESTABLISHED: Circa 1930

NUMBER OF HOLES: 18

COURSE LENGTH/PAR: Back: 3,824/64

COURSE RATING/SLOPE: Back: 59.0/86

HEAD PROFESSIONAL: Yes

COURSE ARCHITECT: Alex Chisholm

GOLF FACILITIES: Full pro shop, practice green, club rental, club repair, club storage, cart rental, pull-cart rental, instruction, locker room, showers, restaurant, lounge, accommodations

TEE TIMES: Not necessary

RANGER: Yes

TEE-OFF INTERVAL TIME: 8 minutes

TIME TO PLAY 18 HOLES: 3 hours, 30 minutes

Earliest Tee-Off: 6 a.m.

Green Fees: Weekend (18): $$ **Weekday (18): $$**

Payment: All major credit cards

Season: April through September

Local Chamber of Commerce: Bath-Brunswick Region, 207-725-8797

Local Attractions: Popham Beach State Park, Maine Maritime Museum

Directions: From Brunswick take Route 1 to Bath. Turn right onto Route 209 and continue to Route 217. The resort is 1 mile ahead on your left.

Course Description: It's been said that nice things come in small packages, which is the case with Shore Acres at Sebasco Harbor Resort. Longtime golf pro Lew Kingsbury describes the course as short and challenging, with lots of character in its small bentgrass greens. The signature hole is the par-3 second—all 113 yards of it. Your tee shot must clear a small saltwater cove (part of Casco Bay, which is visible from several holes) to a large two-tiered green. The eighth hole, which runs 200 yards from its elevated tee, looks out over a 39-acre freshwater pond just behind the green. The course is fairly level throughout, with small bunkers around most greens; a pond comes into play on the dogleg-right ninth hole. The resort is planning an expansion to 18 holes. Work will start on a second nine following the reconfiguration of holes one through six on the front. This is a very family-friendly resort with a large pool, restaurant, and other amenities.

Courses Nearby: Bath, Brunswick, Mere Creek

South Portland Municipal Golf Course

155 Wescott Road

South Portland

207-775-0005

Region: Greater Portland Area

Map: 3

Established: 1975

Number of Holes: 9

Course Length/Par: Back: 4,142/66

Course Rating/Slope: Back: 59.0/92

Head Professional: Yes

Course Architect: NA

Golf Facilities: Club rental, pull-cart rental, snack bar

Tee Times: Not necessary

Ranger: No

Time to Play 18 Holes: 3 hours, 30 minutes

Earliest Tee-Off: 6:30 a.m.

Green Fees: Weekend (18): $ Weekday (18): $

Payment: Cash only

Season: April 15 till first snow

LOCAL CHAMBER OF COMMERCE: Greater Portland Region, 207-772-2811

LOCAL ATTRACTIONS: Greater Portland, Portland Head Light, beaches

DIRECTIONS: Take the Maine Turnpike (I-95) to Exit 6A. Follow I-295 to Exit 3. Take Westbrook Street (Route 9) east to Wescott Road on your left.

COURSE DESCRIPTION: A city course, South Portland Municipal is short but with some subtle challenges. Holes range in length from 122 to 372 yards, the longest being the par-5 fifth, a double dogleg that plays first uphill and then downhill to the green. Trees nearly surround the putting surface. There is no sand or water, making this course ideal for beginners.

COURSES NEARBY: Gorham, Nonesuch River, Pleasant Hill, Riverside Municipal, Sable Oaks, Willowdale

SPRING MEADOWS GOLF & COUNTRY CLUB
ROUTE 100
GRAY
207-657-2585
WEB: www.colefarms.com

REGION: Greater Portland Area

MAP: 5

ESTABLISHED: 1999

NUMBER OF HOLES: 9 (full 18 to open in 2000)

COURSE LENGTH/PAR: Back: 6,622/72   **Middle:** 6,113/72   **Front:** 4,922/72

COURSE RATING/SLOPE: Back: NA   **Middle:** NA   **Front:** NA

HEAD PROFESSIONAL: Yes

COURSE ARCHITECT: W. Bradley Booth

GOLF FACILITIES: Full pro shop, practice green, practice bunker, club rental, club repair, cart rental, pull-cart rental, instruction, locker room, showers, restaurant, snack bar, lounge

TEE TIMES: Recommended

HOW LONG IN ADVANCE: 7 days

RANGER: Yes

TEE-OFF INTERVAL TIME: 12 minutes

TIME TO PLAY 18 HOLES: 4 hours

EARLIEST TEE-OFF: 7:00 a.m.

GREEN FEES: Weekend (18): $$ **Weekday (18): $$**

PAYMENT: All major credit cards

SEASON: April through October

LOCAL CHAMBER OF COMMERCE: Greater Portland Region, 207-772-2811

LOCAL ATTRACTIONS: Greater Portland area, Sebago Lake

DIRECTIONS: Take Exit 11 off the Maine Turnpike. Turn right onto Route 100 North. The course is 1 mile ahead on your left.

COURSE DESCRIPTION: Designed by Ogunquit-based architect W. Bradley Booth (see The Ledges and The Meadows), nine holes opened in the fall of 1999. The full 18 holes will be in play by late summer 2000. A unique layout according to Booth who says rolling hills and grassy wetlands give the impression you're in the lowlands of South Carolina. Built by the same family that owns Cole Farms Restaurant across the street.

COURSES NEARBY: Fairlawn, Frye Island, Poland Spring, Val Halla, Point Sebago

SPRINGBROOK GOLF CLUB
ROUTE 202
LEEDS
207-946-5900
WEB: www.springbrook.com
REGION: Kennebec/Moose River Region
MAP: 12
ESTABLISHED: 1966
NUMBER OF HOLES: 18
COURSE LENGTH/PAR: Back: 6,408/71   **Middle:** 6,163/71   **Front:** 4,989/74
COURSE RATING/SLOPE: Back: 70.4/127   **Middle:** 69.2/125   **Front:** 70.8/123
HEAD PROFESSIONAL: Yes
COURSE ARCHITECT: Al Biondi
GOLF FACILITIES: Full pro shop, driving range, practice green, practice bunker, club rental, club repair, cart rental, pull-cart rental, instruction, locker room, showers, restaurant, lounge
TEE TIMES: Necessary on weekends and holidays
HOW LONG IN ADVANCE: 1 week
RANGER: Yes
TEE-OFF INTERVAL TIME: 8 minutes
TIME TO PLAY 18 HOLES: 4 hours
EARLIEST TEE-OFF: 7:00 a.m.
GREEN FEES: Weekend (18): $$ **Weekday (18): $$**
PAYMENT: MasterCard, Visa
SEASON: Mid-April through mid-November
LOCAL CHAMBER OF COMMERCE: Androscoggin County, 207-783-2249
LOCAL ATTRACTIONS: Greater Lewiston-Auburn area, Great Falls Balloon Festival, Thorncrag Bird Sanctuary
DIRECTIONS: Take Exit 8 off the Maine Turnpike (I-95) and travel east on Route 202 through Auburn and Lewiston. The course is approximately 18 miles ahead on your right.
COURSE DESCRIPTION: A former cattle farm, this rural course features rolling hills, a meandering stream, and beautiful wildflowers. Noted for its challenging greens and top conditioning the course has been the site of several Maine Opens. Because of the hilly terrain, blind shots and sidehill lies add to the challenge. The signature hole is the 210-yard par-3 fifteenth—uphill to a small elevated green protected by bunkers and generally swirling winds. Designer Al Biondi likes to

tell the story of how he laid out the course yardage by hitting 5-irons. But many locals feel that when he got to the fifteenth, he must have snuck in a driver, or at least had a hurricane wind at his back. A huge ravine on the 480-yard par-5 sixteenth must be negotiated if you plan to reach the green in two. Although the course appears open, tall grass, bunkers, and hazards make Springbrook a good links-style test. Wildflowers add to its beautiful country setting. The spacious restaurant/lounge occupies the former post-and-beam cattle barn.

COURSES NEARBY: Apple Valley, Cobbossee Colony, Prospect Hill, The Meadows, Turner Highlands

SQUAW MOUNTAIN VILLAGE GOLF COURSE

ROUTE 15

GREENVILLE JUNCTION

207-695-3609

REGION: Katahdin/Moosehead Region

MAP: 41

ESTABLISHED: Circa 1925

NUMBER OF HOLES: 9

COURSE LENGTH/PAR: Back: 4,926/68

COURSE RATING/SLOPE: Back: 62.4/104

HEAD PROFESSIONAL: No

COURSE ARCHITECT: John Parsons (R), John Shirley (R)

GOLF FACILITIES: Practice green, club rental, club storage, cart rental, pull-cart rental

TEE TIMES: Not necessary

RANGER: Yes

TIME TO PLAY 18 HOLES: 2 hours, 30 minutes

EARLIEST TEE-OFF: 7 a.m.

GREEN FEES: Weekend (18): $ Weekday (18): $

PAYMENT: Cash only

SEASON: Memorial Day through Columbus Day

LOCAL CHAMBER OF COMMERCE: Moosehead Lake Region, 207-695-2702

LOCAL ATTRACTIONS: Moosehead Lake, Squaw Mountain, hiking, camping

DIRECTIONS: From Exit 39 (Newport) off I-95 follow Route 7 North to Dexter. Turn left on Route 23 North and continue to Guilford. Turn left onto Route 15 North to Greenville. From Greenville follow Route 15 for 3 miles. The course is on your right.

COURSE DESCRIPTION: A very scenic course and located directly on Moosehead Lake. Golf has been played here since the turn of the century, but the course was not formally organized until the 1920s. Big Squaw Mountain Ski Area is visible from several holes. This is a short layout, but narrow, tree-lined fairways make for an interesting challenge. Small greens and some hilly terrain. The 310-yard par-4 first parallels the lake. Moose are a common sight in this area.

COURSES NEARBY: Mount Kineo

STREAMSIDE GOLF COURSE
ROUTE 139
WINTERPORT
207-223-9009
REGION: Mid-Coast Region
MAP: 22
ESTABLISHED: 1998
NUMBER OF HOLES: 9
COURSE LENGTH/PAR: Back: 5,820/72   Front: 5,160/72
COURSE RATING/SLOPE: Back: 64.4/99   Front: NA
HEAD PROFESSIONAL: No
COURSE ARCHITECT: Galen Wellman
GOLF FACILITIES: Club rental, club storage, cart rental, pull-cart rental
TEE TIMES: Not necessary
RANGER: No
TIME TO PLAY 18 HOLES: 3 hours, 30 minutes
EARLIEST TEE-OFF: 7 a.m.
GREEN FEES: Weekend (18): $ Weekday (18): $
PAYMENT: Cash only
SEASON: April through September
LOCAL CHAMBER OF COMMERCE: Bangor Region, 207-947-0307
LOCAL ATTRACTIONS: Swan Lake, Fort Knox (Bucksport)
DIRECTIONS: From Belfast take Route 1 North to Route 1A (toward Bangor). In Frankfort turn left onto Loggin Road where 1A makes sharp right. Follow Loggin to its end, then turn right onto Route 139. The course is on your left.
COURSE DESCRIPTION: Streamside was reopened in 1998 by new owners after being abandoned for 20 years. The layout has been reorganized and a few new holes added. The course is not as open as it may first appear. The first and second holes parallel Marsh Stream, which gives the course its name. As such, these   fairways slope toward the woods and water. Greens on both holes are tucked right up against woods and stream. Because of the rolling terrain, only the tops of the pins are visible on the approach. The remaining holes are relatively flat, but trees tighten a few approaches. There is a small pro-shop building with limited facilities.
COURSES NEARBY: Bucksport, Country View, Hampden, Searsport Pines

SUGARLOAF/USA GOLF CLUB
ROUTE 27
CARRABASSETT VALLEY
207-237-6812
WEB: www.sugarloaf.com
REGION: Western Lakes and Mountains

MAP: 29

ESTABLISHED: 1985

NUMBER OF HOLES: 18

COURSE LENGTH/PAR: Back: 6,910/72   **Middle:** 6,451/72   **Front:** 5,376/72

COURSE RATING/SLOPE: Back: 74.4/151   **Middle:** 72.3/146   **Front:** 73.7/136

HEAD PROFESSIONAL: Yes

COURSE ARCHITECT: Robert Trent Jones Jr.

GOLF FACILITIES: Full pro shop, driving range, practice green, practice bunker, club rental, club repair, club storage, cart rental, pull-cart rental, instruction, golf school, restaurant, lounge, accommodations

TEE TIMES: Necessary

HOW LONG IN ADVANCE: 2 weeks

RANGER: Yes

TEE-OFF INTERVAL TIME: 10 minutes

TIME TO PLAY 18 HOLES: 4 hours, 30 minutes

EARLIEST TEE-OFF: 6 a.m.

GREEN FEES: Weekend (18): $$$$ Weekday (18): $$$$

PAYMENT: All major credit cards

SEASON: Mid-May through October

LOCAL CHAMBER OF COMMERCE: Sugarloaf Area, 207-235-2100

LOCAL ATTRACTIONS: Sugarloaf Mountain, Stanley Museum, wildlife, hiking

DIRECTIONS: From Portland take Exit 12 off the Maine Turnpike (I-495). Follow Route 4 to Farmington, then take Route 27 to Kingfield. A large sign identifies Sugarloaf/USA's access road about 8 miles from town on your left. The golf course road is the first right.

COURSE DESCRIPTION: Located in ski country, Sugarloaf/USA is perennially ranked as one of the best golf courses in all of New England. It is easily the most challenging course in the state (playing to a slope of 151 from the tips) and certainly one of the best maintained. This Robert Trent Jones Jr. design features numerous doglegs; narrow, unforgiving fairways; and large, well-bunkered, undulating greens, all cut through thickly wooded mountainous terrain. But what this course presents in difficulty is more than made up for by its sheer beauty. Holes ten and eleven—the most photographed in the state—are prime examples. Both start from elevated tees, as in 150 feet above the fairway. Just getting to the 200-yard par-3 eleventh tee along the switchbacked cart path is an adventure. But the view from the tee looking across to Bigelow Mountain 8 miles to the north is spectacular. The boulder-strewn Carrabassett River comes into play here and for the next four holes — part of Sugarloaf's heralded String of Pearls — but never more dramatically, perhaps, than at the 370-yard fourteenth, where it winds its formidable girth across the front of the green. Sugarloaf is definitely one of Maine's must-play courses—just bring lots of golf balls. Sugarloaf is home to The Orginal Golf School. Stay-and-play packages are available.

COURSES NEARBY: Lakewood, Mingo Springs

Summit Golf Course
White Oak Hill
Poland
207-998-4515
Region: Western Lakes and Mountains
Map: 5
Established: 1920
Number of Holes: 14
Course Length/Par: Back: 5,655/72
Course Rating/Slope: Back: 67.2/115
Head Professional: No
Course Architect: Alex Findlay (O9), Wilfred Leonard
Golf Facilities: Practice green, cart rental, pull-cart rental, snack bar
Tee Times: Not necessary
Ranger: No
Time to Play 18 Holes: 4 hours
Earliest Tee-Off: 7 a.m.
Green Fees: Weekend (18): $ Weekday (18): $
Payment: Cash only
Season: April through September
Local Chamber of Commerce: Androscoggin County, 207-783-2249
Local Attractions: Range Ponds State Park, Shaker Museum
Directions: From Portland take Exit 11 off the Maine Turnpike. Follow Route 26 to Poland, turning left onto White Oak Hill Road. The second left is Summit Spring Road.
Course Description: Currently at 14 holes, Summit is a family-owned golf course that is expanding one hole at a time. The original front nine traverses the top of Oak Hill, with some great views of the White Mountains. Formerly farmland, these hilltop holes are flat and fairly wide open with small greens. The new holes are being cut through woods and present an altogether different set of problems. Narrow and tree lined, these holes play down the side of the hill, with creative doglegs and water hazards providing the excitement.
Courses Nearby: Fairlawn, Point Sebago, Poland Spring, Prospect Hill

Todd Valley Country Club
282 Bacon Road
Charleston
207-285-7725
Region: Katahdin/Moosehead Region
Map: 32
Established: 1970
Number of Holes: 9

COURSE LENGTH/PAR: Back: 4,736/66 **Front:** 4,042/66
COURSE RATING/SLOPE: Back: 61.1/93 **Front:** NA
HEAD PROFESSIONAL: No
COURSE ARCHITECT: Donovan Todd
GOLF FACILITIES: Driving range, practice green, club rental, club repair, pull-cart rental
TEE TIMES: Not necessary
RANGER: No
TIME TO PLAY 18 HOLES: 3 hours, 30 minutes
EARLIEST TEE-OFF: Sunrise
GREEN FEES: Weekend (18): $ Weekday (18): $
PAYMENT: Cash only
SEASON: Snowmelt till snowfall
LOCAL CHAMBER OF COMMERCE: Southern Piscataquis County, 207-564-7533
LOCAL ATTRACTIONS: Kenduskeag Stream
DIRECTIONS: From Bangor take Exit 48 off I-95. Follow Route 15 North toward Charleston. Just past the junction with Route 11A, take a left onto Bacon Road. The course is 1 mile ahead.
COURSE DESCRIPTION: This is an open, rolling, links-style course that plays along a mountain ridge. Built to the lay of the land, the 150-yard par-3 sixth hole has been likened to a Coney Island roller coaster. Short par-4s are the rule, but the small, sloping greens make tough targets. There are exceptional views in all directions from the 250-yard seventh green. Todd Valley has no members, no tournaments, and no leagues; this is golf at its purest. Presently 9 holes, there is a plan to expand the course to 18 "soon."
COURSES NEARBY: Dexter Municipal, Foxcroft, Hidden Meadows, Katahdin, Kenduskeag Valley, Whitetail

TURNER HIGHLANDS COUNTRY CLUB
ROUTE 117
TURNER
207-224-7060
REGION: Western Lakes and Mountains
MAP: 11
ESTABLISHED: 1993
NUMBER OF HOLES: 18
COURSE LENGTH/PAR: Back: 6,039/71 **Front:** 4,726/71
COURSE RATING/SLOPE: Back: 68.6/115 **Front:** 66.1/113
HEAD PROFESSIONAL: No
COURSE ARCHITECT: Steve Leavitt
GOLF FACILITIES: Full pro shop, driving range, practice green, club rental, club storage, cart rental, pull-cart rental, instruction, locker room, showers, restaurant

TEE TIMES: Recommended

HOW LONG IN ADVANCE: 7 days

RANGER: Yes

TEE-OFF INTERVAL TIME: 10 minutes

TIME TO PLAY 18 HOLES: 4 hours, 30 minutes

EARLIEST TEE-OFF: 6 a.m.

GREEN FEES: Weekend (18): $$ **Weekday (18): $$**

PAYMENT: All major credit cards

SEASON: Early May through early November

LOCAL CHAMBER OF COMMERCE: Androscoggin County, 207-783-2249

LOCAL ATTRACTIONS: Great Falls Balloon Festival, apple picking and cider pressings, Norland Living History Center

DIRECTIONS: In Turner turn right onto Route 117. The course is 8 miles ahead on your right.

COURSE DESCRIPTION: This course is set along a ridge amid a working apple orchard, with a few holes cut into thick woodlands. The woodland holes are much tighter, and sloping fairways often make it hard to keep a ball in play. But these holes are softened by the broader ridgetop holes that feature gently rolling hills and wonderful western views of the mountains in New Hampshire. The locally infamous fifth is one of the more unusual par-4s you'll encounter in the state. At just 365 yards, it's a good lesson in course management. A pond sits about 180 yards off the tee. Just beyond the pond's far edge there's a 40-foot sheer drop to the green, which is fronted by a small stream. If that's not enough, the putting surface, closely surrounded by trees, slopes sharply from back to front. Most members confess to laying up in front of the pond, again just before the drop-off, and then trying to place a wedge onto the green and hoping to one-putt. Bogey here is considered a good score. Comfortable, modern clubhouse and golf shop. Great place to play during apple season.

COURSES NEARBY: Apple Valley, Maple Lane Inn, Norway, Paris Hill, Prospect Hill, Springbrook

TWIN FALLS GOLF CLUB

364 SPRING STREET

WESTBROOK

207-854-5397

REGION: Greater Portland Area

MAP: 5

ESTABLISHED: 1970

NUMBER OF HOLES: 9

COURSE LENGTH/PAR: Back: 4,880/66

COURSE RATING/SLOPE: Back: 61.3/90

HEAD PROFESSIONAL: No

COURSE ARCHITECT: Albert Young, Richard Young

GOLF FACILITIES: Club rental, cart rental, pull-cart rental, snack bar

TEE TIMES: Not necessary

RANGER: No

TIME TO PLAY 18 HOLES: 4 hours

EARLIEST TEE-OFF: 7 a.m.

GREEN FEES: Weekend (18): $ Weekday (18): $

PAYMENT: Cash only

SEASON: April through October

LOCAL CHAMBER OF COMMERCE: Greater Portland Region, 207-772-2811

LOCAL ATTRACTIONS: Greater Portland area, Maine Mall

DIRECTIONS: From Portland take Exit 7 off the Maine Turnpike (I-95). Turn left onto Cummings Road, then right onto Spring Street. The course is about 2½ miles ahead on your right.

COURSE DESCRIPTION: A short but challenging track on the outskirts of Greater Portland. A former dairy farm, its rolling terrain and small greens give this layout its character. The longest hole is the 408-yard par-4 fifth (there are no par-5s here). Typical of shorter courses, its par-3s stand out. Water comes into play on two of them, the 165-yard second and the 185-yard sixth. A bunker in front of the green and woods left and right with a severe drop off the back make the 137-yard third a tough target. Changes are in the works at Twin Falls: Three holes are being reconstructed and lengthened to make this a par-70 layout (for 18 holes). The new holes will be completed by 2001. The farm's converted dairy barn serves as the clubhouse.

COURSES NEARBY: Gorham, Rivermeadow, Riverside, Val Halla, Westerly Winds

VA JO WA GOLF COURSE

WALKER ROAD
ISLAND FALLS
207-463-2128

REGION: Aroostook

MAP: 52

ESTABLISHED: 1964

NUMBER OF HOLES: 18

COURSE LENGTH/PAR: Back: 6,423/72   **Middle:** 6,062/72   **Front:** 5,065/72

COURSE RATING/SLOPE: Back: 70.4/125   **Middle:** 69.1/121   **Front:** 69.6/115

HEAD PROFESSIONAL: Yes

COURSE ARCHITECT: Vaughn Walker, Warren Walker

GOLF FACILITIES: Full pro shop, driving range, practice green, practice bunker, club rental, cart rental, instruction, lounge

TEE TIMES: Recommended

HOW LONG IN ADVANCE: One week

RANGER: Yes

TEE-OFF INTERVAL TIME: 8–10 minutes

TIME TO PLAY 18 HOLES: 4 hours, 15 minutes

EARLIEST TEE-OFF: 7 a.m.

GREEN FEES: Weekend (18): $$ **Weekday (18):** $$

PAYMENT: MasterCard, Visa, Discover

SEASON: May through October

LOCAL CHAMBER OF COMMERCE: Northern Katahdin Valley, 207-463-2077

LOCAL ATTRACTIONS: Lakes, fishing

DIRECTIONS: From Bangor take I-95 North to Exit 59. Go east on Route 2 for 3 miles to Pond Road. Take the first right onto Walker Road.

COURSE DESCRIPTION: One of southern Aroostook County's most popular golf venues, Va Jo Wa was rated one of Maine's top public golf courses in the 1997 *New England Golf Guide*. Family owned and operated, this course is well maintained and regularly draws golfers from as far away as Bangor (just an hour and 20 minutes to the south). Sloping terrain and great views of nearby mountains and Mount Katahdin to the west characterize the layout, which runs along the top of a ridge. The front nine is relatively open compared to the back, where trees narrow the fairways. Highlighting the front is the short par-3 sixth. At 102 yards, it might appear tame, but the water behind a severely sloping green means getting on—and, more important, staying on—is a tall order. The 491-yard par-5 eighteenth is a great finisher. A dogleg left, the approach is downhill to a small green with water to the right, a bunker left, and out of bounds just beyond. Good course management will help you play well here.

COURSES NEARBY: Hillcrest, Houlton Community

VAL HALLA GOLF CLUB

1 VAL HALLA ROAD

CUMBERLAND

207-829-2225

REGION: Greater Portland Area

MAP: 5

ESTABLISHED: 1965

NUMBER OF HOLES: 18

COURSE LENGTH/PAR: Back: 6,567/72   **Middle:** 6,201/72   **Front:** 5,437/72

COURSE RATING/SLOPE: Back: 71.1/126   **Middle:** 69.6/122   **Front:** 71.4/120

HEAD PROFESSIONAL: Yes

COURSE ARCHITECT: Philip Wogan

GOLF FACILITIES: Full pro shop, driving range, practice green, practice bunker, club rental, cart rental, pull-cart rental, instruction, showers, restaurant, lounge

TEE TIMES: Necessary

HOW LONG IN ADVANCE: 1 week for weekday, 2 days for weekend

RANGER: Yes

TEE-OFF INTERVAL TIME: 8 minutes

TIME TO PLAY 18 HOLES: 4 hours, 30 minutes

EARLIEST TEE-OFF: 7 a.m.

GREEN FEES: Weekend (18): $$$ **Weekday (18): $$**

PAYMENT: MasterCard, Visa

SEASON: April 15 through October 31

LOCAL CHAMBER OF COMMERCE: Greater Portland Region, 207-772-2811

LOCAL ATTRACTIONS: Greater Portland area, Cumberland Fair, L. L. Bean

DIRECTIONS: Take Exit 6 off the Maine Turnpike to I-295, then Exit 10 (Falmouth-Cumberland) off I-295. Take a right off the ramp. At a stop sign take a right onto Route 9, and follow it through Cumberland Center. Turn right onto Greely Road. Val Halla Road is on your right.

COURSE DESCRIPTION: Opened originally as a privately owned public course, Val Halla was sold to the town of Cumberland in the 1970s. A second nine was added by Phil Wogan (designer of the original nine) in the 1980s. The resulting layout is a mixture of tight, tree-lined holes with open, more forgiving ones. The 142-yard par-3 second requires a carry over a pond from the elevated tee to a tree-ringed green whose front edge hugs the edge of a steep incline that slopes into the pond. Back-to-back par-5s at the 538-yard thirteenth and 440-yard fourteenth offer nice blend of risk-and-reward options. The eighteenth, a sharp 398-yard dogleg right, has a short landing area, leaving a challenging approach into a green that has a brook just in front. It's a memorable finishing hole.

COURSES NEARBY: Freeport, Gorham, Riverside Municipal, Rivermeadow, Sable Oaks, Spring Meadows, Twin Falls

WATERVILLE COUNTRY CLUB

COUNTRY CLUB ROAD

WATERVILLE

207-465-9861

REGION: Kennebec/Moose River Region

MAP: 21

ESTABLISHED: 1916

NUMBER OF HOLES: 18

COURSE LENGTH/PAR: Back: 6,427/70   **Middle:** 6,108/70   **Front:** 5,381/73

COURSE RATING/SLOPE: Back: 69.6/124 **Middle:** 68.2/121   **Front:** 71.3/119

HEAD PROFESSIONAL: Yes

COURSE ARCHITECT: Orrin Smith (O9), Geoffrey Cornish, William Robinson

GOLF FACILITIES: Full pro shop, driving range, practice green, practice bunker, club rental, club repair, club storage, cart rental, pull-cart rental, instruction, locker room, showers, restaurant, lounge

TEE TIMES: Necessary

How Long in Advance: Day of play

Ranger: No

Tee-Off Interval Time: 8 minutes

Time to Play 18 Holes: 4 hours

Earliest Tee-Off: 7 a.m.

Green Fees: Weekend (18): $$$$ **Weekday (18): $$$$**

Payment: Cash only

Season: April 10 through November 10

Local Chamber of Commerce: Mid-Maine, 207-873-3315 or 3316

Local Attractions: Colby College

Directions: From Augusta take I-95 North to Exit 33. Turn left off the ramp. Country Club Road is 1 mile ahead on your left.

Course Description: The original nine here was designed by Orrin Smith, who began his career as a construction superintendent for Willie Park Jr. and later was associated with Donald Ross on several projects. Ranked by *Golf Digest* as one of the top courses in the state, Waterville Country Club is a regular host of the Maine Amateur. Fairways are flat and lined by heavy rough. Most holes reward the straight tee shot and a good short game. Greens are well bunkered, undulating, and fast. This is not a particularly long course, but it's certainly challenging. Take the short par-4 seventh, for example. It's just 300 yards but with a large pond stretching across the fairway just in front of the green—which slopes toward the water and is protected on the left and behind by bunkers—the approach is anything but a breeze. Similarly, the approach on the 410-yard dog-leg-right eighth is uphill to a good-size, two-tiered green. If the pin is back, it's hard to hold the ball on the upper shelf, making three putts a distinct possibility.

Courses Nearby: Belgrade Lakes, Cedar Springs, Natanis, Pine Ridge

WAWENOCK COUNTRY CLUB
Route 129

Walpole

207-563-3938

Region: Mid-Coast Region

Map: 7

Established: 1928

Number of Holes: 9

Course Length/Par: Back: 6,037/70   **Front:** 5,680/74

Course Rating/Slope: Back: 69.0/120   **Front:** 73.5/119

Head Professional: Yes

Course Architect: Stiles & Van Kleek

Golf Facilities: Full pro shop, driving range, practice green, practice bunker, club rental, club repair, club storage, cart rental, pull-cart rental, instruction, locker room, showers, snack bar

TEE TIMES: Necessary

HOW LONG IN ADVANCE: 1 week

RANGER: Yes

TEE-OFF INTERVAL TIME: 8 minutes

TIME TO PLAY 18 HOLES: 4 hours

EARLIEST TEE-OFF: 8 a.m.

GREEN FEES: Weekend (18): $$ Weekday (18): $$

PAYMENT: MasterCard, Visa, Discover

SEASON: Mid-April through October 31

LOCAL CHAMBER OF COMMERCE: Damariscotta Region, 207-563-8340

LOCAL ATTRACTIONS: Pemaquid Beach, Rachel Carson Salt Pond Preserve

DIRECTIONS: From Brunswick take Route 1 North to Damariscotta. Turn right onto Route 129. The course is about 6 miles ahead on your right.

COURSE DESCRIPTION: Located on a peninsula well off the beaten path, Wawenock qualifies as one of Maine's classic hidden gems. It was designed by Wayne Stiles and John Van Kleek in 1928; the original blueprint of their proposed 18-hole layout hangs in the clubhouse. The course plays into a valley and up the other side. The pastoral view from the fifth green looking back across the course to the pillared clubhouse and nineteenth-century meetinghouse next door is something out of a Currier & Ives painting. As peaceful as the setting is the course is by no means tranquil. Typical of Stiles & Van Kleek, the 398-yard second is a dogleg right that plays uphill to a narrow green. Cutting the corner is not an option, leaving a long second shot to a tough target. An elevated tee helps on the 233-yard par-3 third but playing uphill to the 134-yard eighth is another story. It's a blind tee shot to a long, narrow, tiered green that has deep, steep-faced bunkers right and left.

COURSES NEARBY: Boothbay

WEBHANNET GOLF CLUB

8 CENTRAL STREET

KENNEBUNK BEACH

207-967-2061

REGION: Southern Coast

MAP: 3

ESTABLISHED: 1910

NUMBER OF HOLES: 18

COURSE LENGTH/PAR: Back: 6,101/70   **Front:** 5,381/73

COURSE RATING/SLOPE: Back: 67.9/112 **Front:** 71.9/120

HEAD PROFESSIONAL: Yes

COURSE ARCHITECT: Eugene Wogan

GOLF FACILITIES: Full pro shop, practice green, practice bunker, club repair, club storage, cart rental, pull-cart rental, instruction, locker room, showers

TEE TIMES: Necessary

HOW LONG IN ADVANCE: 24 hours

RANGER: Yes

TEE-OFF INTERVAL TIME: 8 minutes

TIME TO PLAY 18 HOLES: 4 hours

EARLIEST TEE-OFF: 9 a.m.

GREEN FEES: Weekend (18): $$$$ Weekday (18): $$$$

PAYMENT: Cash only

SEASON: May through October

LOCAL CHAMBER OF COMMERCE: Kennebunk-Kennebunkport, 207-967-0857

LOCAL ATTRACTIONS: Beaches, Kennebunkport area

DIRECTIONS: From Exit 3 off the Maine Turnpike (I-95) take Route 35 East to Sea Road. Turn right onto Sea Road and proceed to Ridge Avenue. Turn left; the course is ½ mile ahead.

COURSE DESCRIPTION: A venerable layout that, as a semiprivate club, offers just six public tee times each day, Webhannet originally opened as a nine-hole course in 1910. New England–based architect Eugene "Skip" Wogan expanded the layout to 18 holes in the 1920s. Except for some minor remodeling, the layout is virtually unchanged from his original design. A links-style course, it is fairly open, with few bunkers guarding the small but undulating greens. The par-3s—the 238-yard third, 175-yard fifth, and 220-yard eleventh—are the favorites here. The fifth is uphill to an elevated and sloping green. Located near Kennebunk Beach, this course's occasional fog and a seemingly ever-present sea breeze add to the challenge. Former Secretary of State Edmund Muskie (under Jimmy Carter) was a longtime member here.

COURSES NEARBY: Biddeford-Saco, Cape Arundel, Dutch Elm, Sanford

WEST NEWFIELD GOLF COURSE

LIBBY ROAD

WEST NEWFIELD

207-793-2478

REGION: Southern Coast

MAP: 2

ESTABLISHED: 1995

NUMBER OF HOLES: 9

COURSE LENGTH/PAR: Back: 3,000/60

COURSE RATING/SLOPE: Back: 55.1/86

HEAD PROFESSIONAL: No

COURSE ARCHITECT: Brian Schindler

GOLF FACILITIES: Practice green, club rental, club storage, cart rental, pull-cart rental, snack bar

TEE TIMES: Not necessary

RANGER: No

TEE-OFF INTERVAL TIME: 10 minutes

TIME TO PLAY 18 HOLES: 2 hours, 30 minutes

EARLIEST TEE-OFF: 7 a.m.

GREEN FEES: Weekend (18): $ Weekday (18): $

PAYMENT: Cash only

SEASON: May through October 12

LOCAL CHAMBER OF COMMERCE: Sanford/Springvale, 207-324-4280

LOCAL ATTRACTIONS: Willowbrook at Newfield, lakes, wildlife

DIRECTIONS: From Exit 2 off the Maine Turnpike (I-95) take Route 109 through Sanford. Turn right onto Route 11, then left onto Route 110. At the intersection of Libby and Stevens Roads, look for a sign.

COURSE DESCRIPTION: This rural executive-style course features three par-4s ranging in length from 250 to 330 yards. Its par-3s are 125 yards or less. Picturesque layout with lots of wildlife.

COURSES NEARBY: Golf at Province Lake, Sanford

WESTERLY WINDS GOLF COURSE
771 CUMBERLAND ROAD
WESTBROOK
207-854-9463

REGION: Greater Portland Area

MAP: 3

ESTABLISHED: 1985

NUMBER OF HOLES: 9 (new 18-hole course planned)

COURSE LENGTH/PAR: Back: 806/54

COURSE RATING/SLOPE: Back: NA

HEAD PROFESSIONAL: Yes

COURSE ARCHITECT: NA

GOLF FACILITIES: Full pro shop, driving range, practice green, practice bunker, club rental, pull-cart rental, instruction, snack bar

TEE TIMES: Not necessary

RANGER: No

TIME TO PLAY 18 HOLES: 2 hours or less

EARLIEST TEE-OFF: 8 a.m.

GREEN FEES: Weekend (18): $ Weekday (18): $

PAYMENT: MasterCard, Visa

SEASON: April 1 through late October

LOCAL CHAMBER OF COMMERCE: Greater Portland Region, 207-772-2811

LOCAL ATTRACTIONS: Greater Portland area, beaches

DIRECTIONS: Take Exit 8 off the Maine Turnpike and continue straight through the first light, turning right at the second one. Pass the S. D. Warren Mill and head toward Windham. The course is 2 miles ahead on your right.

COURSE DESCRIPTION: This short par-3 course features rolling terrain with some trees. Holes range in length from 60 to 160 yards. Part of a sports complex that includes baseball batting cages, swimming pool, tennis courts, miniature golf, and shuffleboard. A new 3,100-yard 9-hole course will open in spring 2000, and plans call for expanding it to a full 18 by 2001.

COURSES NEARBY: Gorham, Sable Oaks, Twin Falls, Val Halla

WESTERN VIEW GOLF CLUB
BOLTON HILL ROAD
AUGUSTA
207-622-5309
REGION: Kennebec/Moose River Region
MAP: 12
ESTABLISHED: 1935
NUMBER OF HOLES: 9
COURSE LENGTH/PAR: Back: 5,410/70   **Front:** 5,260/72
COURSE RATING/SLOPE: Back: 64.5/107 **Front:** NA
HEAD PROFESSIONAL: Yes
COURSE ARCHITECT: NA
GOLF FACILITIES: Full pro shop, driving range, practice green, practice bunker, club rental, cart rental, pull-cart rental, instruction, snack bar
TEE TIMES: Not necessary
RANGER: Yes
TIME TO PLAY 18 HOLES: 3 hours, 30 minutes
EARLIEST TEE-OFF: 7 a.m.
GREEN FEES: Weekend (18): $ Weekday (18): $
PAYMENT: MasterCard, Visa
SEASON: April till snowfall
LOCAL CHAMBER OF COMMERCE: Kennebec Valley, 207-623-4559
LOCAL ATTRACTIONS: Greater Augusta area, state capitol, government offices
DIRECTIONS: From Augusta take Exit 30 off I-95, then head east on Route 100/201. Cross the Kennebec River and turn right onto Route 105. About 4 miles ahead, take a left onto Bolton Road. The course is at the top of the hill on your left.

COURSE DESCRIPTION: Traversing the side of Bolton Hill to the east of Augusta, Western View is a short course with some of the smallest greens in Maine. Its hillside setting presents some interesting challenges. At 445 yards, the par-5 fifth—longest hole on the course—plays uphill along the edge of the ridgeline that once served as the starting point of a long-abandoned ski hill. Tall trees define the corner on the downhill sharp dogleg-right 300-yard par-4 seventh. A rock outcropping—one of many throughout the course—marks the left side. A loyal membership helps give this club its character.

COURSES NEARBY: Belgrade Lakes, Capitol City, Cobbossee Colony, Kennebec Heights, Natanis

WHITE BIRCHES GOLF CLUB
ROUTE 1
ELLSWORTH
207-667-3621
REGION: Acadia/Down East
MAP: 24
ESTABLISHED: 1983
NUMBER OF HOLES: 18
COURSE LENGTH/PAR: NA
HEAD PROFESSIONAL: Yes
COURSE ARCHITECT: NA
GOLF FACILITIES: Full pro shop, practice green, practice bunker, club rental, cart rental, pull-cart rental, instruction, restaurant, snack bar, lounge, accommodations
TEE TIMES: Not necessary
TIME TO PLAY 18 HOLES: 3 hours
EARLIEST TEE-OFF: 7 a.m.
GREEN FEES: Weekend (18): $ Weekday (18): $
PAYMENT: All major credit cards
SEASON: April through October
LOCAL CHAMBER OF COMMERCE: Ellsworth Area, 207-667-5584
LOCAL ATTRACTIONS: Mount Desert Island, Acadia National Park
DIRECTIONS: Take Route 1 to Ellsworth; the course is about 2 miles north of town on your left.
COURSE DESCRIPTION: A former 9-hole layout currently being rebuilt into an 18-hole par-3 track. Holes will range in length from 100 to 190 yards. Plans call for tree-lined fairways, tiered greens, and lights. A motel and a restaurant are on site, and an RV park is planned as well. Will be open for the 2000 season.
COURSES NEARBY: Bar Harbor, Grindstone Neck, Lucerne-in-Maine

WHITETAIL GOLF COURSE

373 SCHOOL ROAD
CHARLESTON
207-285-7730
REGION: Katahdin/Moosehead Region
MAP: 32
ESTABLISHED: 1997
NUMBER OF HOLES: 9
COURSE LENGTH/PAR: Back: 5,276/68   **Front:** 4,794/68
COURSE RATING/SLOPE: Back: 63.4/104 **Front:** NA
HEAD PROFESSIONAL: No
COURSE ARCHITECT: Scott Duthie
GOLF FACILITIES: Pro shop, practice green, practice bunker, club rental, club repair, cart rental, pull-cart rental, restaurant
TEE TIMES: Not necessary
RANGER: No
TIME TO PLAY 18 HOLES: 3 hours, 30 minutes
EARLIEST TEE-OFF: 7 a.m.
GREEN FEES: Weekend (18): $ Weekday (18): $
PAYMENT: Cash only
SEASON: April 15 through October 15
LOCAL CHAMBER OF COMMERCE: Southern Piscataquis County, 207-564-7533
LOCAL ATTRACTIONS: Lakes
DIRECTIONS: From Exit 48 off I-95 take Route 15 North. The course is about 10 miles from Kenduskeag.
COURSE DESCRIPTION: About 20 miles from Bangor, this short nine-hole layout is one of two golf courses in Charleston, population 800. Owner designed, the course offers a little of everything. The first few holes are wide open—starting with the 493-yard par-5 first—but then become less forgiving. The 245-yard par-4 fourth plays downhill a right-to-left-sloping green. Though the green is reachable locals say this hole is "an easy four or a hard other." Set on top of a hill, the course is picturesque offering views of Bangor and beyond.
COURSES NEARBY: Dexter Municipal, Foxcroft, Katahdin, Kenduskeag Valley, Todd Valley

WILLOWDALE GOLF CLUB

52 WILLOWDALE ROAD
SCARBOROUGH
207-883-9351
REGION: Greater Portland Area
MAP: 3
ESTABLISHED: 1940s

NUMBER OF HOLES: 18

COURSE LENGTH/PAR: Back: 5,980/70 **Front:** 5,344/70

COURSE RATING/SLOPE: Back: 67.9/110 **Front:** NA/112

HEAD PROFESSIONAL: No

COURSE ARCHITECT: Eugene Wogan

GOLF FACILITIES: Full pro shop, practice green, club rental, club repair, club storage, cart rental, pull-cart rental, locker room, showers, snack bar, lounge

TEE TIMES: Recommended on weekends and holidays

HOW LONG IN ADVANCE: 3 days

RANGER: Yes

TEE-OFF INTERVAL TIME: 8 minutes

TIME TO PLAY 18 HOLES: 4 hours

EARLIEST TEE-OFF: 6 a.m.

GREEN FEES: Weekend (18): $$ **Weekday (18): $$**

PAYMENT: MasterCard, Visa, Discover

SEASON: April through October

LOCAL CHAMBER OF COMMERCE: Greater Portland Region, 207-772-2811

LOCAL ATTRACTIONS: Scarborough Downs, Maine Mall, beaches, parks

DIRECTIONS: Take the Maine Turnpike (I-95) to Exit 6. Drive straight through the light, then follow the road to its end. Turn left onto Route 1. Willowdale Road is the first right.

COURSE DESCRIPTION: Convenient to downtown Portland and area beaches, Willowdale's picturesque layout features two distinct nine-hole loops. The earlier front side is relatively flat, with broad fairways defined by well-established pine trees and subtly sloped greens. The 375-yard fourth and 195-yard fifth hole border the 3,100-acre Scarborough Marsh. The latter requires a tee shot over wetland that runs up the left side to a good-size target with trees and a bunker to the right. Be sure to pause for a moment to take in the view from the green back across the marsh before heading on to the next tee. The back side is tighter and, because of its rolling fairways, presents several blind shots and uneven lies. The 405-yard par-4 tenth sets the tone. Tee off over a stream to a uphill landing area. The long approach is over a deep gully to a sloped green. The modern clubhouse is spacious, comfortable, and a friendly place to relax after your round.

COURSES NEARBY: Biddeford-Saco, Dunegrass, Dutch Elm, Gorham, Nonesuch River, Old Orchard, Pleasant Hill, Riverside, Sable Oaks, Salmon Falls, South Portland

WILSON LAKE COUNTRY CLUB
WELD ROAD—ROUTE 156
WILTON

207-645-2016

WEB: www.Route2.com/wlcc.htm

REGION: Western Lakes and Mountains

MAP: 19

ESTABLISHED: 1935

NUMBER OF HOLES: 9

COURSE LENGTH/PAR: Back: 6,159/70   **Front:** 5,614/74

COURSE RATING/SLOPE: Back: 68.8/117 **Front:** 71.9/119

HEAD PROFESSIONAL: Yes

COURSE ARCHITECT: Stiles & Van Kleek

GOLF FACILITIES: Full pro shop, practice green, practice bunker, club rental, club repair, club storage, cart rental, pull-cart rental, instruction, locker room, snack bar

TEE TIMES: Recommended

RANGER: Yes

TEE-OFF INTERVAL TIME: 8 minutes

TIME TO PLAY 18 HOLES: 4 hours

EARLIEST TEE-OFF: 6:30 a.m.

GREEN FEES: Weekend (18): $$ **Weekday (18): $**

PAYMENT: MasterCard, Visa

SEASON: May 1 through October 31

LOCAL CHAMBER OF COMMERCE: Wilton Community, 207-645-3932

LOCAL ATTRACTIONS: Wilson Pond, Mount Blue State Park, University of Maine—Farmington

DIRECTIONS: From Auburn take Exit 12 off the Maine Turnpike (I-495), then take Route 4 North to Wilton. Turn left onto Route 156 toward Weld. The course is 2 miles ahead.

COURSE DESCRIPTION: A classic nine-holer located in Maine's western mountains. Designed by Wayne Stiles and John Van Kleek in 1931, this 6,159-yard layout is well maintained and little changed over the past decades. Old-style mounded bunkers guard the greens and give this course a classic feel. The 215-yard par-3 eleventh is considered by many the best par-3 in the state. The large green is well bunkered both right and left. Tall pines along the hole frame its beauty and add a quality of danger to the tee shot. The green has some tricky breaks that will challenge you through your last putt.

COURSES NEARBY: Oakdale, Maple Lane Inn, Sandy River

GOLF SCHOOLS

ROLAND STAFFORD GOLF SCHOOL
BETHEL INN & COUNTRY CLUB
BETHEL
800-447-8894
WEB: www.bethelinn.com

MAINE GOLF ACADEMY JUNIOR GOLF CAMP
2720 TAYLOR WOODS ROAD
BELGRADE
888-GOLF-CAMP
WEB: www.golfcamp.com

POINT SEBAGO GOLF SCHOOLS
POINT SEBAGO GOLF COURSE & RESORT
CASCO
207-655-2747
WEB: www.pointsebago.com

SAMOSET RESORT GOLF SCHOOL
SAMOSET RESORT GOLF CLUB
ROCKPORT
207-594-2511
800-341-1650 (OUTSIDE MAINE)
WEB: www.samoset.com

THE ORIGINAL GOLF SCHOOL
SUGARLOAF/USA GOLF CLUB
CARRABASSETT VALLEY
800-843-5623
WEB: www.sugarloaf.com

＊　＊　＊　＊

GOLF ASSOCIATIONS

MAINE STATE GOLF ASSOCIATION
374 US ROUTE 1
YARMOUTH, MAINE 04096
207-846-3800
FAX: 207-846-4055
WEB: www.mesg.org

MAINE GOLF COURSE SUPERINTENDENTS ASSOCIATION
170 US ROUTE 1, SUITE 200
FALMOUTH, ME 04105
207-781-7878
FAX: 207-781-2866
WEB: www.mgcsa.com

GOLF MAINE
304 GORHAM ROAD
SCARBOROUGH, ME 04074
800-636-8562
WEB: www.golfme.com

NEW ENGLAND PROFESSIONAL GOLFERS ASSOCIATION (NEPGA)
284 EAST TEMPLE STREET
P.O. BOX 743
BOYLSTON, MA 01505
508-869-0000
FAX: 508-869-0009
E-MAIL: neweng@pgahq.com

MAINE CHAPTER—NEPGA
2 HOUSTON LANE
BREWER, ME 04412
207-989-4631

MAINE GOLF HALL OF FAME
P.O. BOX 8142
PORTLAND, ME 04104-8142
PHONE/FAX: 207-799-0983

*   *   *   *

GOLF PUBLICATIONS

MAINE GOLF MAGAZINE
P.O. BOX 289
HALLOWELL, ME 04347
207-623-8060
FAX: 207-623-6097
E-MAIL: MeGolfInc@aol.com
WEB: www.mainegolfmagazine.com

TravelGolf Maine
P.O. Box 130
Rockport, ME 04856
207-236-6716
Fax: 207-230-0354
E-mail: info@travelgolfmaine.com
Web: www.travelgolfmaine.com

*   *   *   *

General Information

Maine Office of Tourism
1-888-624-6369
Web: www.visitmaine.com

*   *   *   *

Golf Courses by Town

City/Town	Golf Course
Albion	Cedar Springs Golf Course
Arundel	Dutch Elm Golf Club
Auburn	Prospect Hill Golf Course
Augusta	Capitol City Golf Course
	Western View Golf Club
Bangor	Bangor Municipal Golf Club
Bar Harbor	Kebo Valley Club
Bath	Bath Country Club
Belgrade Lakes	Belgrade Lakes Golf Course
Berwick	Links at Outlook
Bethel	Bethel Inn & Country Club
Boothbay	Boothbay Country Club
Brewer	Pine Hill Golf Club
Bridgton	Bridgton Highlands Country Club
Brooks	Country View Golf Club
Brunswick	Brunswick Golf Club
	Mere Creek Golf Course
Bucksport	Bucksport Golf Course
Burnham	Lakeview Golf Club
Calais	St. Croix Country Club

CAPE NEDDICK	CAPE NEDDICK COUNTRY CLUB
CARIBOU	CARIBOU COUNTRY CLUB
CARMEL	CARMEL VALLEY GOLF LINKS
CARRABASSETT VALLEY	SUGARLOAF/USA GOLF CLUB
CASCO	POINT SEBAGO GOLF COURSE & RESORT
CASTINE	CASTINE GOLF CLUB
CHARLESTON	TODD VALLEY COUNTRY CLUB
	WHITETAIL GOLF COURSE
CUMBERLAND	VAL HALLA GOLF CLUB
DENMARK	ALLEN MOUNTAIN GOLF COURSE
DEXTER	DEXTER MUNICIPAL GOLF CLUB
DOVER-FOXCROFT	FOXCROFT GOLF CLUB
ELLSWORTH	WHITE BIRCHES GOLF CLUB
ENFIELD	GREEN VALLEY GOLF CLUB
FARMINGDALE	KENNEBEC HEIGHTS COUNTRY CLUB
FARMINGTON FALLS	SANDY RIVER GOLF COURSE
FORT FAIRFIELD	AROOSTOOK VALLEY COUNTRY CLUB
FORT KENT	FORT KENT GOLF CLUB
FREEPORT	FREEPORT COUNTRY CLUB
FRYE ISLAND	FRYE ISLAND GOLF CLUB
GORHAM	GORHAM COUNTRY CLUB
GRAY	SPRING MEADOWS GOLF & COUNTRY CLUB
GREENVILLE JUNCTION	SQUAW MOUNTAIN VILLAGE GOLF COURSE
GUILFORD	PISCATAQUIS COUNTRY CLUB
HAMPDEN	HAMPDEN COUNTRY CLUB
HERMON	HERMON MEADOWS GOLF CLUB
HOLDEN	FELT BROOK GOLF CENTER
HOLLIS	SALMON FALLS COUNTRY CLUB
HOULTON	HOULTON COMMUNITY GOLF COURSE
ISLAND FALLS	VA JO WA GOLF COURSE
JACKMAN	MOOSE RIVER GOLF CLUB
KENDUSKEAG	KENDUSKEAG VALLEY GOLF COURSE
KENNEBUNK BEACH	WEBHANNET GOLF CLUB
KENNEBUNKPORT	CAPE ARUNDEL GOLF COURSE
LEEDS	SPRINGBROOK GOLF CLUB
LEWISTON	APPLE VALLEY GOLF CLUB
LIMESTONE	LIMESTONE COUNTRY CLUB
LINCOLN	JATO HIGHLANDS GOLF CLUB
LITCHFIELD	THE MEADOWS GOLF CLUB
LIVERMORE FALLS	MAPLE LANE INN & GOLF CLUB
LOVELL	LAKE KEZAR COUNTRY CLUB

LUCERNE-IN-MAINE	**LUCERNE-IN-MAINE GOLF COURSE**
MADISON	**LAKEWOOD GOLF CLUB**
MARS HILL	**MARS HILL COUNTRY CLUB**
MEXICO	**OAKDALE GOLF CLUB**
MILLINOCKET	**HILLCREST GOLF CLUB**
MILO	**KATAHDIN COUNTRY CLUB**
MONMOUTH	**COBBOSSEE COLONY GOLF COURSE**
NAPLES	**NAPLES GOLF CLUB**
NEWPORT	**ORCHARD VIEW GOLF CLUB**
NORTH HAVEN	**NORTH HAVEN GOLF CLUB**
NORTHEAST HARBOR	**NORTHEAST HARBOR GOLF CLUB**
NORTHPORT	**NORTHPORT GOLF CLUB**
NORWAY	**NORWAY COUNTRY CLUB**
OLD ORCHARD BEACH	**DUNEGRASS GOLF CLUB**
	OLD ORCHARD BEACH COUNTRY CLUB
OLD TOWN	**HIDDEN MEADOWS GOLF COURSE**
ORONO	**PENOBSCOT VALLEY COUNTRY CLUB**
PALMYRA	**PALMYRA GOLF COURSE**
PARIS	**PARIS HILL COUNTRY CLUB**
PARSONFIELD	**GOLF AT PROVINCE LAKE**
PITTSFIELD	**J. W. PARKS GOLF COURSE**
POLAND	**FAIRLAWN GOLF & COUNTRY CLUB**
	SUMMIT GOLF COURSE
POLAND SPRING	**POLAND SPRING COUNTRY CLUB**
PORTAGE	**PORTAGE HILLS COUNTRY CLUB**
PORTLAND	**RIVERSIDE MUNICIPAL GOLF COURSE**
PRESQUE ISLE	**PRESQUE ISLE COUNTRY CLUB**
RANGELEY	**MINGO SPRINGS GOLF COURSE**
ROCKLAND	**ROCKLAND GOLF CLUB**
ROCKPORT	**GOOSE RIVER GOLF CLUB**
	SAMOSET RESORT GOLF CLUB
ROCKWOOD	**MOUNT KINEO GOLF COURSE**
ROQUE BLUFFS	**GREAT COVE GOLF CLUB**
SACO	**BIDDEFORD-SACO GOLF CLUB**
SANFORD	**PINE HOLLOW LITTLE PAR 3**
	SANFORD COUNTRY CLUB
SCARBOROUGH	**NONESUCH RIVER GOLF CLUB**
	PLEASANT HILL GOLF CLUB
	WILLOWDALE GOLF CLUB
SEARSPORT	**SEARSPORT PINES GOLF COURSE**
SEBASCO ESTATES	**SHORE ACRES GOLF CLUB**

SKOWHEGAN	LOONS COVE GOLF COURSE
SORRENTO	BLINK BONNIE GOLF CLUB
SOUTH PORTLAND	SABLE OAKS GOLF CLUB
	SOUTH PORTLAND MUNICIPAL GOLF COURSE
SOUTHWEST HARBOR	CAUSEWAY GOLF CLUB
ST. DAVID	BIRCH POINT GOLF CLUB
SUNSET	ISLAND COUNTRY CLUB
TRENTON	BAR HARBOR GOLF CLUB
TURNER	TURNER HIGHLANDS COUNTRY CLUB
VASSALBORO	NATANIS GOLF CLUB
WALPOLE	WAWENOCK COUNTRY CLUB
WATERVILLE	PINE RIDGE MUNICIPAL GOLF COURSE
	WATERVILLE COUNTRY CLUB
WEST NEWFIELD	WEST NEWFIELD GOLF COURSE
WESTBROOK	RIVERMEADOW GOLF CLUB
	TWIN FALLS GOLF CLUB
	WESTERLY WINDS GOLF COURSE
WILTON	WILSON LAKE COUNTRY CLUB
WINTER HARBOR	GRINDSTONE NECK GOLF COURSE
WINTERPORT	STREAMSIDE GOLF COURSE
YORK	HIGHLAND LINKS GOLF CLUB
	THE LEDGES GOLF CLUB

*　　*　　*　　*

GOLF COURSES BY SLOPE

THE FOLLOWING SLOPE RATINGS ARE FROM THE REGULAR MEN'S TEES.

146	SUGARLOAF/USA GOLF CLUB
135	THE LEDGES GOLF CLUB
134	SABLE OAKS GOLF CLUB
133	BELGRADE LAKES GOLF COURSE
130	BETHEL INN & COUNTRY CLUB
130	KEBO VALLEY CLUB
130	POINT SEBAGO GOLF COURSE & RESORT
126	PENOBSCOT VALLEY COUNTRY CLUB
125	SAMOSET RESORT GOLF CLUB
125	SPRINGBROOK GOLF CLUB
124	GOLF AT PROVINCE LAKE
123	BATH COUNTRY CLUB
123	BRIDGTON HIGHLANDS COUNTRY CLUB

102	KATAHDIN COUNTRY CLUB
102	PARIS HILL COUNTRY CLUB
102	ST. CROIX COUNTRY CLUB
99	FELT BROOK GOLF CENTER
99	STREAMSIDE GOLF COURSE
97	ISLAND COUNTRY CLUB
93	TODD VALLEY COUNTRY CLUB
92	PINE HILL GOLF CLUB
92	SOUTH PORTLAND MUNICIPAL GOLF COURSE
90	CAUSEWAY GOLF CLUB
90	TWIN FALLS GOLF CLUB
87	PLEASANT HILL GOLF CLUB
86	SHORE ACRES GOLF CLUB
86	WEST NEWFIELD GOLF COURSE
84	GREAT COVE GOLF CLUB

THE FOLLOWING COURSES DO NOT CURRENTLY HAVE SLOPE RATINGS:

BIRCH POINT GOLF CLUB
CAPITOL CITY GOLF COURSE
CARMEL VALLEY GOLF LINKS
GRINDSTONE NECK GOLF COURSE
LOONS COVE GOLF COURSE
MOOSE RIVER GOLF CLUB
MOUNT KINEO GOLF COURSE
ORCHARD VIEW GOLF CLUB
PINE HILL GOLF CLUB
PINE HOLLOW LITTLE PAR 3
PINE RIDGE MUNICIPAL GOLF COURSE
SANDY RIVER GOLF COURSE
SPRING MEADOWS GOLF & COUNTRY CLUB
WESTERLY WINDS GOLF COURSE
WHITE BIRCHES GOLF CLUB

*   *   *   *

PRIVATE COURSES

ABENAKEE CLUB, ST. MARTIN'S LANE, BIDDEFORD, ME, 207-283-3811
AUGUSTA COUNTRY CLUB, ROUTE 202, MANCHESTER, ME, 207-623-9624
BLUE HILL COUNTRY CLUB, BLUE HILL, ME, 207-374-2271

CHEBEAGUE ISLAND GOLF CLUB, WHARF ROAD, CHEBEAGUE ISLAND, ME, 207-846-9478

FALMOUTH COUNTRY CLUB, ONE CONGRESSIONAL DRIVE, FALMOUTH, ME, 207-878-2864

MARTINDALE COUNTRY CLUB, BEECH HILL ROAD, AUBURN, ME, 207-782-9074

MEGUNTICOOK GOLF CLUB, CALDERWOOD LANE, ROCKPORT, ME, 207-236-2666

PORTLAND COUNTRY CLUB, 11 FORESIDE ROAD, FALMOUTH, ME, 207-781-3053

PROUTS NECK COUNTRY CLUB, PROUTS NECK, SCARBOROUGH, ME, 207-883-9851

PURPOODOCK COUNTRY CLUB, SPURWINK AVENUE, CAPE ELIZABETH, ME, 207-799-0821

TARRATINE GOLF CLUB, GOLF CLUB ROAD, DARK HARBOR, ME, 207-734-2248

WOODLANDS COUNTRY CLUB, 39 WOODS ROAD, FALMOUTH, ME, 207-781-3104

YORK GOLF & TENNIS CLUB, 214 ORGANUG ROAD, YORK, ME, 207-363-2683